PRAISE FOR PAUL BRUNTON AN

"A powerful transmission for our time. *Instructions for Spiritual Living* and Paul Brunton's lifetime works should continue to inspire the world for years to come. This powerful book bridges ancient and modern mysticism. A gem!"

MARIANA CAPLAN, PH.D., MFT, AUTHOR OF *HALFWAY UP THE MOUNTAIN: THE ERROR OF PREMATURE CLAIMS TO ENLIGHTENMENT*

"A truly comprehensive and authoritative work that should be read by sincere seekers and advanced adepts alike. Paul Brunton's work demonstrates a real mastery of the intricacies of spiritual life. His sagely conclusions on a number of key topics rarely covered elsewhere in spiritual literature provide an important contribution to our contemporary understanding of awakening and enlightenment. This kind of knowledge is indispensable for the modern seeker, because it provides a clear picture of not only what to expect when going through the process of dis-identifying with form and becoming one with the formless but also how to properly integrate this profound transformation of consciousness into an ordinary human life. We are very fortunate that his writings are available."

STEPHEN D'AMICO, AUTHOR OF *HEAVEN ON EARTH* AND *THE INCREDIBLE STATE OF ABSOLUTE NOTHINGNESS*

"Paul Brunton's wisdom is like the child's voice in the story "The Emperor's New Clothes." His observations and spiritual insights reveal a laser-sharp eye that directs us back to that which is obvious within us, though obviously overlooked—the Divine Self."

MOOJI, SPIRITUAL TEACHER

"Paul Brunton was surely one of the finest mystical flowers to grow on the wasteland of our secular civilization. What he has to say is important to us all."

GEORG FEUERSTEIN (1947–2012), AUTHOR OF *THE YOGA-SUTRA OF PATAÑJALI*

"In *The Short Path to Enlightenment,* Paul Brunton gives voice to the profound teachings of immediate spiritual awakening that have the power to short circuit the seeker in us and reveal the true nature of reality here and now. But the true gift of this wonderful book is in how nuanced and subtle Paul Brunton understood these profound and transformational teachings and how directly he conveys them. Read this book as you would a scripture or a sutra and let it open your eyes to eternity."

ADYASHANTI, AUTHOR OF *THE WAY OF LIBERATION*

"The Short Path to Enlightenment is a deeply supportive text from the extraordinary Paul Brunton, the spiritual explorer who first brought knowledge of Ramana Maharishi to the West. In this work, readers receive the invitation and instruction to discover the truth of oneself. This book is alive with supreme knowledge. May it support you in immediately and continually recognizing yourself."

GANGAJI, AUTHOR OF *THE DIAMOND IN YOUR POCKET*

"With the possible exception of Alan Watts, Paul Brunton has probably been the most influential exponent of Eastern philosophy and systems of self-realization in this century. . . . significant commentaries on nearly every conceivable aspect of the spiritual quest . . . unreservedly recommended as the final, eloquent summing up by one of the West's most perceptive thinkers and deepest students of the ancient wisdom."

THE AMERICAN THEOSOPHIST

"Nowhere else will you find such a profound synthesis of East-West philosophic mysticism stripped of all the usual obscurity and extravagances. Both the modern intellect and the weary heart will find unlimited inspiration, wisdom, and guidance for action in these Notebooks."

VICTOR MANSFIELD (1941–2008),
AUTHOR AND PROFESSOR OF PHYSICS AND ASTRONOMY
AT COLGATE UNIVERSITY

"Paul Brunton's Notebooks series is a veritable treasure trove of philosophic-spiritual wisdom."

ELISABETH KUBLER-ROSS (1926–2004),
AUTHOR OF *ON DEATH AND DYING*

INSTRUCTIONS
FOR
SPIRITUAL
LIVING

· ·
· ·

PAUL BRUNTON

EDITED BY JEFF COX

Inner Traditions
Rochester, Vermont

Inner Traditions
One Park Street
Rochester, Vermont 05767
www.InnerTraditions.com

Originally published in the United Kingdom in 1984 by Rider & Company under the title *Essays on the Quest*

First U.S. edition (paperback) published in 1985 by Samuel Weiser under the title *Essays on the Quest*

Revised and expanded second edition published in 2019 by Inner Traditions under the title *Instructions for Spiritual Living*

Chapter 9, "The Working of Grace," was originally published in 1986 by Larson Publications in *The Notebooks of Paul Brunton: Practices for the Quest/Relax and Retreat,* volume 3, in chapter 9, "Conclusion," beginning on page 216. It is reprinted here with permission.

Appendix, "My Initiations into the Overself," was originally published in 1987 by Larson Publications in *The Notebooks of Paul Brunton: Reflections on My Life and Writings,* volume 8, in chapter 1, "Two Essays," beginning on page 7. It is reprinted here with permission.

Cataloging-in-Publication Data for this title is available from the Library of Congress

ISBN 978-1-62055-804-1 (print)
ISBN 978-1-62055-805-8 (ebook)

Printed and bound in the United States by McNaughton & Gunn, Inc.

10 9 8 7 6 5 4 3 2 1

Text design by Priscilla H. Baker and layout by Virginia Scott Bowman
This book was typeset in Garamond Premier Pro with Futura and Kurry Eco used as display typefaces

For more information on the Paul Brunton Philosophic Foundation and the author of this book, mail a first-class letter to the foundation c/o Inner Traditions • Bear & Company, One Park Street, Rochester, VT 05767, and we will forward the communication, or contact the foundation directly at **www.paulbrunton.org**.

Contents

Introduction
by the Paul Brunton Philosophic Foundation   ix

ONE
The Adventure of Meditation   1

TWO
Is the Soul in the Heart?   38

THREE
The Interior Word   44

FOUR
Self-Reliance or Discipleship?   51

FIVE
Ethical Qualifications of the Seeker   89

SIX
Cleansing of the Emotions   95

SEVEN
Surrender of the Ego   116

EIGHT
The Probations and Tests of the Aspirant   129

NINE
The Working of Grace   149

TEN
Insight   159

ELEVEN
Is the World an Illusion?   172

TWELVE
Ascetic Mysticism Reconsidered   183

THIRTEEN
What Can We Do for Philosophy?   203

APPENDIX
My Initiations into the Overself   215

Other Works by Paul Brunton
and Related Works   234

Index   237

PB is one of my "eyes." My Shakti [spiritual power] is working through him. Follow him closely.

Ramana Maharshi

Introduction

By the Paul Brunton Philosophic Foundation

INSTRUCTIONS FOR SPIRITUAL LIVING examines both foundational and advanced topics central to most spiritual paths. Whether we have a teacher or not, spiritual development is fraught with complexities and challenges. Paul Brunton offers transformative wisdom that aids our understanding of what the spiritual journey entails and helps point the way when the way is uncertain.

"PB," as he preferred to be called, was a gentle man from whom an aura of peace and kindness emanated. His deep understanding of the spiritual life was forged in the crucible of experience, and his spiritual depth shines through his writings.

PB provides instructions to guide one's development in three fundamental areas: in a full course of the stages of meditation to deepen one's inner life; in a process of self-examination that roots obstacles out of one's character; and in the unfolding of full awakening that includes wisdom in action. As he makes clear, the living expression of realization is a life of service both to the inner wellspring of wisdom as well as to others.

Beginning with "The Adventure of Meditation," the first chapters open the door to the inner landscape. Meditation is the art and practice of introverting attention, of freeing oneself for a period of time from the thoughts, sensations, and feelings that are usually at the center of our attention, and allowing the Soul to reveal itself out of the quiet that one has created. PB guides us with insight and care through the stages of concentration, meditation, and contemplation. He explains the goal of each stage and the obstacles that are likely to arise in the process of achieving each. Invaluable are the pointers and encouragement he gives us to continue with patience as we strive to deepen our practice. The chapters: "Is the Soul in the Heart" and "The Interior Word" are marvelous supplements to our understanding and experience of the inner life.

Undoubtedly, there is great need for instruction in the spiritual pursuit. However, PB examines, questions, and challenges the need for dependency on any particular person, organization, teaching, or practice in his chapter "Self-Reliance or Discipleship?" After all is said and done, we are striving to realize our essence and inner wisdom—our lives are *individual* expressions of that essential wisdom, and because of this often-overlooked fact, PB explains and emphasizes the necessity and value of the independent path.

In the next few chapters, PB lays out the ethical qualifications and emotional purifications that are integral to our progress toward self-realization. It is our attachments that bar the door to our Soul and block our search for truth, and a steady dose of self-examination is critical for our success in spiritual life. Striving to understand our nature, and the aspiration that makes this process an enlivening one, awakens our intuition. Following intuition aligns us with our ideals, and thereby prevents us from succumbing to emotional disturbances and temptations. Realization requires the surrender of egoistic fixations so that we may attend to the inspiration flowing from within, which PB refers to as "grace." In "The Probations and Tests of the Aspirant," he proffers an eye-opening explanation of how life's challenges are moments by which we can make real progress in our surrender to a higher life.

While a primary goal of mystical meditation is the realization of our inner reality in a sense-free and thought-free contemplation, it is the development of transcendental insight that enables the realization of this reality whether we are awake, a'dream, or asleep. In the chapter on "Insight," PB refers to a person who has achieved this realization as a "philosopher" (by elevating its meaning to "lover of Truth/Reality"). He explains:

> Mystics find their inner self. They discover that personality is rooted in a deeper, wider being—the Overself. But they do not discover the significance of the not-self. They do not enter into comprehension of the All. Once a philosophic illumination has been gained, it shines steadily and enduringly. It is never clouded even for a moment. In other words, the philosopher walks in perpetual light and not in intermittent flashes of light as does the mystic. The philosophic knowledge is a well-established one, whereas the mystic knowledge is an occasional one. Philosophic truth is a constant and unclouded power of the one, whereas fleeting intuition or temporary ecstasy at best is the attainment of the other.

Insight is the cornerstone of compassionate wisdom in action and, once achieved, enables us to become a source of inspiration to all whom we encounter. In the final chapters, he elaborates how the philosopher's orientation to life is one of altruistic service, a constant call to enlighten others.

In an appendix, we have included PB's candid account of his spiritual unfoldment, which he wrote for the purpose of providing a living example of the transformational operation and power of these teachings and especially to inspire and encourage anyone who is drawn to study and practice them.

Instructions for Spiritual Living has been created from essays that were unpublished during PB's lifetime. The Paul Brunton Philosophic Foundation selected them from the large archive of PB's writings and arranged them to form this manual for spiritual practice and realization.

Please note that Paul Brunton wrote in the mid-twentieth century when the literary convention was to use "he" rather than "he or she," but PB intended that these teachings applied to everyone interested in them. The editors have updated PB's language to reflect this fact and have made some other minor editorial changes to the original text.

The PAUL BRUNTON PHILOSOPHIC FOUNDATION (PBPF) was formed in the mid-1980s after the death of Paul Brunton. PB's son Kenneth Hurst, his literary heir, helped form the PBPF for the purpose of archiving, publishing, and making available the teachings of PB in a variety of media and languages. From PB's archive, a sixteen-volume collection of his previously unpublished writings, *The Notebooks of Paul Brunton,* was created; these volumes have been recognized as a major contribution to spiritual literature, as have his earlier works, which continue to serve as key spiritual resources for generations of seekers. The foundation is based in the Finger Lakes Region of New York and has a twelve-member working board of volunteers who manage its many tasks. For more information about the foundation and PB's work please visit **www.paulbrunton.org.**

ONE

The Adventure of Meditation

IT HAS BEEN CUSTOMARY for learned professors of the metaphysics of psychology to teach that consciousness always implies a relation to an object because it is always directed toward something. While this is true, it is true only of the level of ordinary experience. It is no longer true on the level of the highest type of mystical experience. Here consciousness can exist without any relation at all for it can be directed toward its own self. This is the one experience that occurs in the mind and that possesses absolutely no correlation with, nor determination by, what is happening in, to, or outside the body at the same time. Therefore, it is itself a demonstration of the falsity of the materialistic view. The world of ordinary experience is not the last possible one. There is a deeper and diviner world, or in Wordsworth's good phrase, an "unknown mode of being," open to our adventuring. We have not yet attained true self-consciousness; we live too completely on the lower level of our existence for that. It is indeed time we take full possession of ourselves.

But the external encounter with mystical statements is one thing;

the personal experience of mystical states is quite another. Mystical theory has to justify itself in mystical experience. This it is quite able to do. Indeed, its practicality can best be proved by such experience. It will then be found that it cannot be easily disposed of as chimerical. For the experience of thousands of people throughout history, situated in every station of life, has confirmed the reality and attainability of the transcendental state. However, by contrast with the total number of people in the world, it is relatively only a few sensitive persons who have heard these mystical overtones of human existence. Yet we should not regard the mystic as a highly specialized type of human being. He or she is like ourselves but has had the vision and patience to follow up an act of faith with a long-drawn series of active experiments to test the truth of that faith. If one individual has touched this higher consciousness, all may touch it. The prerogative is not exclusive but inclusive, not personal but common.

There is something in us of which we are not normally conscious. It is only at rare moments that we become aware—and that dimly—of a second self, as it were, of a nobler and serener self. We may have experienced such an uplift for only a few minutes but we will be haunted forever afterward by a sense of its tremendous importance. For we sense that we have then been in contact with something other than our ordinary self, sublimer than our ordinary self, yet despite that somehow related to it. Those of us who have passed through such an inspired mood, who have felt its serenity, tasted its power, and obeyed its monitions, know well enough that only then have we been fully alive. Against the adamantine fact of our own overwhelming experience, the barbed arguments of others' skepticism avail nothing. There is no substitute for it. It is beyond all intellectual scholarship, above all religious rites.

This is indeed nothing other than the recognition of the "Soul." The Soul is most certainly there but if we do not turn inward and attend to it, then for us it is not there. But really it is always there and the failure to recognize its existence is really the failure to turn attention away from the endless multitude of things that continuously extrovert it. This is why meditation, which is the art of introverting attention, is so needful. By means of our own mind, we can discover the Soul. The introverted consciousness, turned away from the five sense activities to contemplate itself, first feels the presence and later becomes aware of the Divine Mind behind it. Therefore, the practice of mental introversion, or meditation, is quite essential on this quest.

We cannot recapture those glorious moments of recognition, yet we cannot forget them. This tantalizing situation imposes a restlessness and disquiet upon our feelings, which will never be assuaged unless and until we take to the quest. If we would be inspired by the Spirit at all times and in all places, we must first let it inspire us at set times and in set places. This is one justification of meditation. For all inspiration rises out of the inward deeps of our nature. We cannot compel it, but we can invite it. We cannot command it, for it commands us. The best way, therefore, to become inspired is to trace it out intuitively to its source, that is, to the Divine Self within us. Meditation will help this unfolding of latent intuition for it is itself an intuitive process.

Mysticism is a territory with which the average person is quite unfamiliar. One enters it, if one does so at all, with a certain uneasiness and a certain hesitancy. Consequently it is a common habit for ignorant critics to sneer at the mystic, who cultivates the power of introspection, as being morbid. But the fact is that if one is a philosophic mystic, one will become a victorious master of introspection rather than its morbid victim. Whoever, by steady practice, has succeeded with the processes of meditation, becomes a living testimony to its indubitable worth. People such as this give in themselves a demonstration that its promised results can be realized, that it is not

a wild dream or fanciful abstraction. If we have never before practiced the art of meditation, surely we cannot use our time to better
purpose than to begin doing so now. Thus, we will introduce a new
rhythm into our life, which will eventually assist us in every imaginable way, which will make possible the improvement of our character
and capacity, our ethics and consciousness, our understanding and
peace, our intuition and sometimes even our fortune. Faithfully practiced, over a sufficient period of time, it will amply repay the effort
given and will confer benefits for which many are longing but few
are finding. There is also the testimony of history, though because
of its confused character our iconoclastic age may deem this of little account. The yoga system was being taught and practiced beside
the Ganges long before Rome had reached its heyday. The Quaker
method of silent "waiting on the Lord" has been practiced during
the modern era in English villages and American cities. A hundred
different forms of mystical technique may be gathered from mysticism's archives by the student who has the time to do so. Out of this
confused collection of ideas it is still possible to extricate some praxis,
definitely common to all of them, for a methodical cultivation of the
inner life.

THE FOUNDATIONS OF MEDITATIVE PRACTICE

A more precise and less poetic description of the art of meditation
than is usually given would better assist the Western novice. Why
should there not be a science of its technical side as already there are
sciences of the technical aspects of so many other arts? The following pages are one contribution toward the attempt to formulate such
a scientific statement.

The need for solitude and time to cultivate the inner life, in both
its metaphysical and mystical phases, is the first imperative. Solitude

is needed because the presence of others definitely disturbs the emptying process. Time is needed because the mind is habitually filled with thoughts of the outer world; it is essential to totally empty the mind of thoughts for a while—regularly, habitually, and deliberately. Without a determined use of willpower, it is, however, hard for most persons to get solitude or find time.

If the one requirement develops partly out of the aspirant's need to be able to concentrate thought without interruption, it also develops partly from the restless mental auras that most people carry about with them. They themselves shrink from being alone and naturally introduce an antipathetic influence wherever solitary meditation is being practiced. Perhaps their terror of solitude arises because it makes them conscious of the spiritual aimlessness and intellectual vacuity of their sojourn on earth. The fear of being alone simply means that one has no inner life at all. The scale of values that lists solitude as a frightful evil to be avoided, or considers the desire for it as an eccentric or even antisocial trait, is materialistic and stupid. The mystic who has learned the art of creative solitude can hear a mental voice in its inner silence. Thus for him or her the loneliness that is maddening for some is enlightening.

For the other requirement, for a certain period each day there must be a separation from all usual physical labors and intellectual activities, a period wherein aspirants can become and remain bodily still and mentally quiet. We must set apart a little time once or twice a day for meditation, just as we set apart some time for eating food. This is indispensable to achieving spiritual progress. It is quite practicable for most people to create a routine that, while satisfying the need of withdrawal for meditation, nevertheless would not interfere with worldly activities and responsibilities.

It is needful periodically to put aside the things of time so as to seek the timeless, to isolate ourselves from the outward world so as to seek an inward one. The psychological purpose of such isolation is to create a new habit and a new attitude. The habit is meditation. The attitude is introversion. We are led to the hard task of reeducating our powers of perception, understanding, and attention. These powers have to be cultivated through a series of regular exercises. This involves self-training in definite work and a long progressive apprenticeship. Meditation is an art that has to be learned by repeated practice like the art of playing a piano. It comes naturally to virtually no one. Its technique requires a skill that has to be learned like that of any other art.

Here the habit-forming tendency of the mind can be an excellent aid. We will gain more by exercises regularly practiced over a period of, say, six months, than by the same exercises done in fits and starts over the same period. Consequently, a fixed time of the day should be appointed for them. The ideal rhythm would be to meditate three times a day in coordination with the rhythm of the sun's movements—at dawn, noon, and dusk. But we cannot arrive at this all at once. It is best to start with a single period and continue with that for months, or even years, until we feel ready to advance and add a second period to it. We will have to work at these two periods, be they dawn and dusk or noon and dusk, for a considerable time before the inner prompting is likely to tell us to take the further step and add the third period. Even then it may not be possible always to adhere faithfully to the program thus laid down. Social necessities, for instance, may compel us to leave out some period or other almost every week. Hence, we must do our best within the limits of our personal circumstances.

Situated as average Westerners usually are, however, a single meditation may be as much as we can conveniently practice each day. This will be enough and satisfactory progress can be made on such a basis. If sunrise or sunset hours are not available for mystical practice, then we may adjust its timing to suit our own convenience. Although the general rule is that meditation is much easier and more effective immediately before a meal, this rule need not always be rigidly followed. If, for example, it is more convenient to practice after partaking of the first meal of the day and if this breakfast be a light one, that will not be a hindrance; or if at any time of the day there is a genuine feeling of hunger, it would be better to satisfy this feeling first and then try to meditate, rather than to be disturbed by it during the practice period. The rule about selecting a time before meals for meditation does not apply to advanced students. In their case, if a contact with the higher element is made during practice, and the latter is then stopped to partake of food where domestic convenience, social necessity, or other circumstances place the time outside their control, they may if they wish resume meditation after the meal and will usually find that the contact is quickly and easily regained.

It will take some time for the mental agitation created by getting immersed in worldly business or personal affairs to subside. Until this happens, the aspirant cannot proceed with the positive work of meditation but rather must engage in the merely negative task of clearing out those distracting memories. This is one reason why in the East the morning period is recommended for such practice. At the beginning of the day one's thoughts and emotions are still undisturbed; hence withdrawal into one's center is then easier. Some, however, may find the morning—with its anticipation of activities yet to be started—unattractive for this purpose and may regard the very fatigue of a hard day's work as an inducement to relax in the evening and seek inner peace. My own rhythm, which developed to accommodate my circumstances as a busy, hard-working man, is as follows: every morning I remember the higher purpose of my life in prayer, be it only for two or three minutes. Every evening I withdraw, if I can, in an hour-long meditation.

If the regular hour for meditation occasionally proves inconvenient, it may be postponed to a later time. Should this be impossible, the practice may be abandoned for that day. If it is possible to hold enduringly to the full period previously laid down as desirable and available for such exercise, this will help to create an advantageous habit. But if on any particular day the fatigue becomes intolerable, then also it will be better to abandon practice for that day. Aside from these fixed times, or perhaps in displacement of them, the intuitive call to abandon every physical labor and every intellectual activity will recur again and again. We should obey it. In the very midst of business affairs or daily work, we may have sudden lapses into inward abstraction. These will ordinarily be quite brief and definitely should be kept so. But they are worth cultivating wherever and whenever they happen to come. If this is done frequently and faithfully, the power to meditate increases.

Although no universally tenable duration may wisely be fixed, for it will always depend on individual circumstances and personal aptitudes, nevertheless it may be said that in most cases full and perfect concentration for two-and-a-half minutes, or full and perfect meditation for forty-two minutes, is quite enough. The preliminaries of clearing all distracting thoughts out of the mind are not included in these figures. Advanced practitioners who are able to enter the third degree, contemplation, are by the tradition of the hidden teaching—both in their own and in society's interests—advised to limit this delightful experience to twenty-six minutes. But as already stated, a rule for all people at all times and in all places would be unwise. Apprentice meditators are easily fatigued and will best proceed by setting themselves easy tasks and short periods. These can be increased gradually as and when the inner prompting bids them do so. Whenever aspirants have advanced to the point where they intuitively feel that a little more time devoted to these exercises would yield great results, they should follow the leading and seek out ways and means to add a quarter-hour, twenty minutes, and so on. This usually happens only at a certain stage of their progress and should be linked to that stage.

"I often think how tenuous is the thread that holds our thoughts together. Hunger, thirst, heat, cold—a touch of any of them and all the aesthetics . . . vanish as by a wand." So writes Robert Gibbings in his travel book, *Coming Down the Wye*. It is precisely this dependence on externals that makes it necessary for the aspirant to shape them into a cooperative rather than let them remain in an obstructive form. We must not be hampered by the physical apparatus of meditation, but neither must we neglect it. Too much light, for instance, is disturbing to meditation. In the daytime, the window curtains should be drawn. In the evening, city dwellers will find that indirect or shaded electric lighting is best.

The first point to be attended to is the place where we propose to practice. It should be one where we can remain undisturbed for the chosen period. Wherever this is possible, the place should also be rural rather than urban, but freedom of choice is seldom available here. We have only to contrast the soothing tranquillity of country life with the jarring bustle of city life to realize where mystics can best attain their purpose. Life in a large city, with traffic constantly passing, is not conducive to meditation. Forests are particularly friendly to aspirants seeking the right atmosphere for deep, peaceful meditations, gardens to aspirants seeking happy mystical ecstasies.

The next point concerns the body. A straight, upright spine with the head erect and in line with it often helps to keep the meditator's attention alert and gives more force to the concentration. We should try to cultivate the habit of sitting during the period as steadily as a figure in a tableau. At first we will find it hard even to keep physically still for the period of practice, harder yet to keep mentally still;

but the old habits of being fidgety or restless do yield eventually to such endeavors. However, it is absurd to elevate this particular suggestion into a rigid universal dogma, as many yogis do. The importance that they attach to a particular bodily posture during meditation is an exaggerated one. They insist on a perfectly erect spine as the prerequisite to success. Yet the Sufi mystics in the Near East and Iran have meditated for a thousand years with head bent toward the chest or with spine so curved as to bring the face close to the knees, or even with a swaying rhythmic forward-and-backward movement. They have not found this a bar to success and have produced attainments fully equal to those of the yogis. Ralph Waldo Emerson, who was the equal of most Eastern mystics and yogis in mystical apprehension and moral reach—and unquestionably the superior of many in intellectual attainments and psychical balance—used a rocking chair at his writing table. Its rhythmic rise and fall helped his work. Now it could have done so not during the physical act of writing—for that would have been interfered with—but only during the intervals of contemplation between such acts. Therefore he was helped and not hindered by its movement. Thirty years ago I personally could not obtain the mystical trance except by lying on my back in bed. Ten years later, that was the one posture that effectively prevented me from obtaining it! Today it makes no difference whether I sit erect, lie recumbent, or droop my head—the concentrated thought of the Beloved is enough to bring the mind unhindered into quick union with the Beloved.

What is the moral of this? The first is that the thought is what matters most, and what happens inwardly in mind and heart is more important than mere outward activity. Why do the great Eastern religions like Islam, Zoroastrianism, and Hinduism prescribe ablutions before prayer? The real intention is to ensure freedom from the mental disturbance resulting from an unclean and hence uneasy body. There is no mystical virtue in cleanliness. Some of the most reputed saints in the West and fakirs in the East have been physically dirty. Many lamas in Tibet do not bathe for months at a time. The real value of cleanliness lies in removing a possible hindrance from mental concentration during prayer. Therefore, all rules relating to the body in relation to prayer or meditation, including those concerning its posture, should not be overrated, idolized, or made coercive.

The second moral is that each of us should choose the bodily posture that best suits us at the time, or that we receive an inner prompting to adopt, and not torment ourselves trying to conform rigidly to some system when we find that system uncomfortable or impossible. The more we can quieten our body and keep it from fidgeting, the better our concentration will become and the sooner its development will proceed. Comfortably seated, adequately relaxed, with nerves and muscles tension-free, our fleshy house must be kept as still as its mental tenant will, in the highest stage, one day likewise be.

We have accomplished this side of the task when we can sit motionless for the prescribed period without moving a limb and without any other signs of bodily fidgeting or mental distraction.

MEDITATIVE CONCENTRATION

It is now necessary to inquire into the nature and object of the concentration here required. Those who equate the word with what ordinarily passes under its name are both wrong and right. It is true that many people who have never even heard of yoga, such as business executives for example, show a well-developed quality of concentration in their work. But this does not bring them any nearer to the knowledge of the inner Self. On the contrary, they use their concentrative power to bind themselves closer to spiritual ignorance, because they use it to sink more strongly into attachment to external things and, quite often, into the belief that Matter is a reality. The kind of concentration inevitably practiced by a business executive is the same in some ways, but vitally different in others, from that deliberately practiced by a mystic. The one is usually animated by a desire to retain or increase earthly possessions, the other by a desire for the Higher Self to take possession of him or her. The one clings throughout to the intellect's working; the other is glad to let it lapse entirely into stillness at a certain point. The one is concentrating on external things of which he or she can form concrete mental images; the other is concentrating on abstract concepts that eventually rise to the imageless plane. That is, the one often extroverts the mind and the other always introverts it—an entirely opposite process. The mystic's effort should be to penetrate more and more into his or her own conscious being. During the earlier phase of this meditation there is a double endeavor, paradoxically to forget and to remember. On the one hand, we have to strain continually to let go of our earthly self and forget it. On the other hand, we have to strain equally hard to take hold of our Higher Self and rediscover its existence, that is, remember our origin.

All ordinary concentration concerns the *form* side of life, not its *essence*. Mystics may not indeed possess a greater concentration than others are able to show at their best, but by giving it *inward* direction they use it to detach themselves from externals, to weaken their belief in Matter's reality, and to become spiritually self-aware. The antennae of their minds must reach out toward that which as yet they can neither feel nor see. This first movement in the mystical exploration of the human consciousness is the sense in which philosophy uses the word *concentration*.

When the mind stops working, the senses automatically follow into inactivity. When the mind's power is completely stilled, as in sleep, we cannot see, hear, feel, taste, or smell. Hence, mentalism says that the mind is the real experiencing agent. Mysticism takes advantage of this scientific fact to evolve a technique whereby thoughts may be brought under full control or even suspended, the sense-reports dimmed or even banished, but yet the mind's power of self-consciousness may be kept alive. The outgoing tendencies of the self are called in through a deliberate effort of will; the attention is gathered up and its habitual direction reversed through introversion, so that the senses' reports become somewhat blurred. Hence, the first working principle of yoga is the diversion of attention and interest from outward things to an idea, a feeling, a series of thoughts, or a mental image, which fill the void thus created. When thoughts are continually fastened to the senses, they keep up a restless rhythm of attraction and repulsion, of pleasure and pain, which imposes itself between us and stable peace. These minutes of mental quiet must be consecrated to suppressing the outgoing direction of thoughts, to turning them inward, and finally to interning them in their ineffable source.

In your innermost being you are already as divine as you are ever likely to be. Hence, no interior training can give you what you already possess, but a suitable training can help to give you the *consciousness* of what you possess. No practical system can develop a Soul for you, for it is already there, but an adequate system can lead you into the awareness of it. And among the meditation exercises that must necessarily stand foremost in such a system, no single one is absolute and indispensable. There is no universal formula for the practice of meditation suited to all people at all times. It is not advantageous to aspirants to repose in the bed of one formula during their whole lifetime. The philosophic ideals of a balanced development and an equilibrated personality would alone forbid it. On the contrary, they will find it necessary to use different exercises at different periods of their mystical career.

The mystical course passes through a spiral-like ascending rhythm so that if, for instance, we began by meditating on defects of character and later dropped that for a more abstract topic, we will one day return to our former practice again, but this time it will be from a higher standpoint, which will yield correspondingly more important gains. We may fix attention on mental pictures or on abstract ideas, on specific themes or on vague feelings, on keen rational thinking, or on the rejection of all thinking whatsoever. All these exercises have one and the same objective. All are approaches to one and the same psychological state. If the approaches differ, this is only because their points of departure are different. We must smile indulgently at those who insist that their particular method is the only effective one, as we must smile tolerantly also at those who limit truth to their small conception of it. Philosophy does not say that the aspirant should not follow such a method, but that we should not follow it to the exclusion of all others. A method or technique that is good for one person may not be good for another. And the methods that well suited the ancient mind may be ill suited to the modern one, while the conditions laid down in former times may be inadequate to the present time.

But whatever exercise we adopt, let us remember four indispensable points. First, our labor must seek to eliminate all thoughts except the thought of its own theme. Second, the more interested we become in what we are thinking of—yes, even the more excited we become about it—the more successful our concentration becomes. The converse of this is also true. Third, the concentration must pass from thinking about its chosen object in a logical way to entering into the object in a fixed, settled way. Fourth, if the first step is to get a thorough grip on our thoughts and feelings, that is to achieve concentration, then the second step is to elevate them above all worldly activities and desires, that is, to achieve meditation. That meditation begins well that begins by fervent prayer or ardent worship. We must approach the divine withinness of our own Self with all possible reverence, putting away the soiled shoes of worldly cynicism at its threshold.

Real meditation is an intuitive process. But the tensions that prevail in the mind usually prevent this intuition from being felt, and still more, from being followed even if felt. If we are going to carry on with the same thoughts, the same cares, and the same hopes that preoccupied our busy hours, we might as well continue with what we were doing before the meditation hour. The first advantage—as it is the first necessity—of meditation is that it shall concern itself with something entirely different. It must lift us out of the stream of personal life. It must, in short, start and end with one theme: the Overself. Hence, we must begin to meditate by withdrawing our thoughts from our own affairs and those of the world, fixing them instead on the object of our quest—the Overself. During these intervals we should cultivate the capacity to place our worldly business at a distance and to calm the outward-rushing emotions. When we "go into silence," when we sit down to meditate, we should first clear all the day's business or occupations out of our mind. When we enter the meditation chamber, we should let the door shut completely not only on the outside world but also on that inside world where trivialities, routine, business affairs, angers, resentments, irritations, and passions are native inhabitants. Equally so, we should let the past go and disdain the future. We are there to engage ourselves in a holier business than that in which the world usually engages, to follow a diviner occupation than the personality's fated round, and to lift our thoughts to higher levels than the wonted one. The renunciation required of us during this period is both external and internal: it must indeed be total. Mothers must put away their children as though they had never been born. Scholars must forget their books as though they had never rested on their shelves. Manufacturers must travel far from their factories as though they belonged to a dead past. Workers must join the ranks of the unemployed as though they had never been elsewhere.

It often happens that failure in meditation is caused by this failure to detach thoughts from the personal affairs of everyday routine. The first remedy is to choose a theme that in itself holds sufficient interest to keep our thoughts tethered to it. The second remedy is rigidly to transfer attention back to this theme every time we become aware of having strayed.

CHALLENGES TO CONCENTRATION

In theory, the attention ought not to deviate for a single second from the thought upon which it is being held. In practice it will certainly do so, for ancient habit has made it restless, intractable, and dissipated. How weak people have become is shown by their widespread incapacity to pass even a half hour in uninterrupted withdrawal from the affairs of their personal individuality and in unremitting communion with their higher individuality. Concentration inexorably demands that the mind shall not think of twenty different things and people in as many minutes. Yet as soon as anyone sits down to meditate, a motley crowd of thoughts will batter at the gates of consciousness. No one except the experienced person, who has practiced for some years and practiced with regularity, determination, and understanding, is likely to be free of this nuisance. These distractions are so persistent and so troublesome that they drive many, if not most, beginners into hopeless despair or utter boredom, and so ultimately drive them away from meditation exercises altogether.

How many people have had this time-wasting experience in meditation: They think for a moment or two about the spiritual theme they have assigned themselves, but it is soon dropped or crowded out by a host of irrelevant thoughts, memories, and anticipations—mostly of a worldly nature. They finally rise with relief from this irksome effort as soon as the allotted period ends. How often must they wait for the feeling of divine contact only to find at the end of the meditation period that it has again failed to manifest itself! How often have they begun with expectancy only to end with despondency, as this tantalizing elusiveness recurs yet again! If others have found the Divine Self by turning inward, they themselves have been unluckier and found only irresponsive emptiness.

Aspirants must be willing to go through these boring preliminaries and endure the depressing unease of these early experiments. There is no escape from them at the present stage. During the meditation, most of the time is frittered away in fighting mental restlessness and emotional distraction. As thought after thought encroaches upon our attention, we must try to brush each one away as it appears and keep vigilant in this matter. It will require a kind of grip upon ourselves, an inner reserve that says, "Thus far but no farther." It is a strenuous exercise to keep the mind in undistracted and undisturbed concentration upon the quest of the free Self. We are habitually so active, so restless, and so extroverted that the reversal of our ways inevitably meets with stiff and stubborn resistance.

Even for the many persons of moderately successful advancement in the art, meditation is not outright smooth sailing. Alas! There are times for them, too, when the meditation period is filled with desertlike aridity, leaving thoughts restless and emotions bored. However, even such periods are not really wasted but teach humility and patience. Although each practice period has no longer to surmount the natural inertia of the extroverted mentality, it still has to over-come anew not only the inner resistance of a turbulent mentality—although this will be far less than with the unpracticed person—but also the added resistance of alien thought conditions and emotional strains temporarily "picked up" during the day's contacts and meetings with others. This, indeed, is one of the added reasons why students of yoga in the East take to solitude and avoid society. All these resistances evoke shadows of depression, even despair, but they can be overcome by using the sword of patience to pierce them. So, unless they can bear the fatigue no longer, they should not impatiently abandon the practice on that occasion as being useless, but should persist—trying the effect of a prayer to the Higher Self to come to their help. After some minutes, or perhaps a longer time, the resistance may melt away of its own accord.

Few of those who sit down to unroll the colored carpet of meditation really succeed in entering the state of mental quiet. That is a positive and later result, whereas the earlier one is negative. The struggle to keep the attention fixed during the preliminary part of a meditation period is intense. Many become disheartened by its difficulty. Yet the more they attempt it, the easier it certainly will become in time. The disciple should recognize that, just as it often takes a certain period of time satisfactorily to embark on some intellectual work, so it takes a certain time to get started with this spiritual work. Only the adept in meditation can obtain immediate results; all others need to work their way gradually toward this goal.

We must accept the fact that these negative preliminaries, which yield no immediate fruit, must needs take up the greater part of our allotted time, and that we should not look for quick results. This cannot be helped. We must cheer ourselves with the thought that the reward of perseverance is expertness, but until then we must learn to wait and work for the agitated mentality to collect and calm itself and stop its whirl of themes and thoughts. We must remind ourselves that if the practice of meditation is most difficult, it is also most essential; that without this unremitting practice being incorporated into our everyday life, it is not possible to succeed in either detaching ourselves from earthly desires or attaching ourselves to the Overself. Here impatience is a sign that the lower self naturally resists the inward drawing toward meditation, for it sees in such a course the ultimate loss of its own sovereignty. If the commonplace qualities of patience and perseverance have any value anywhere, it is here. With their help and with devotion to the practice, we may, after a protracted period of trial and error, become possessed of a good technique. It was no less a master of the art than the renowned Indian sage Shankara, who said that if meditation is carried on with perseverance and fervor, it will attain its goal in not too long a time.

All the powerful and predominant tendencies that make both the movement of thoughts and the externalization of attention the ingrained habits that they really are, assail us and draw us back to the common enslaved condition in which we and all humankind have hitherto dwelt. Our duty is to summon our inner strength to resist the return of these thoughts and to repel the intrusion of objects upon our attention. The effort to maintain the introverted state must be sustained, not in a violent nor self-conscious way but in an easy and gentle fashion. And it must be repeated day after day without remission until success is complete and permanent. Many beginners make the error of believing that the result, if any, of each individual meditation must necessarily show itself at the time of practice, and of assuming that because the end of a meditation leaves them as they were at the beginning, because it seems barren, dry, and without result, that therefore it is a disappointing failure. This is not so, for the result may show itself a little later and the effort is not wasted; it is only that the profit has not appeared above the threshold of consciousness. These exercises may make the going seem slow and laborious; they must be looked upon as a kind of gymnastic discipline, a self-training whose results in self-development will surely show themselves, although at an unspecifiable date.

Just as we do not discard a mirror because we cannot see our face in it the first time we look, but rub and polish it again and again until we do, so should we not discard the regular practice of meditation because we do not see our Spiritual Self in it the first year, but should persevere until we do. To hush the outgoing energies of the body, to stand aside from the active functioning of the senses, and to bid the waves of thought be still, is a task that naturally calls for a great concentration of all our forces. Therefore it is not an easy one, but nevertheless it is not impossible. Hundreds of men and women have successfully accomplished it during the past centuries and in different lands. The secret of this achievement is not to give up the quest because results remain monotonously absent, not to cease efforts through impatience, irritation, or despair. In the early stages, meditation feels arduous and profitless. In the intermediate stages, there are periods of conscious progress with intervals of staleness. For it is then that the mind works on the pneumatic drill principle. Persevering endeavor will bring proficiency, irregularly no doubt but to an ever-increasing extent. If the thinking consciousness resents these daily attacks upon its restless wandering character and stubbornly clings to its old habits, one day its resistance will be worn out and it will quietly yield.

For months and perhaps years, practitioners will have to draw attention forcibly back from these wanderings, but if we persist the day will surely come when it will stop them of its own accord and willingly seek the rest that meditation offers. The hour will eventually arrive when we will no longer have to try to meditate; meditation will come to us of itself, facilely and smoothly. Expertness in the art of meditation comes, as in all other arts, through this untiring practice. The concentration becomes easy and pleasant. The proficient's internal tension disappears and the whole being becomes well poised, harmoniously relaxed.

THREE STAGES

In this development there are three stages: first, the long, monotonous, tiring fight against the wandering tendencies of the intellect; second, the shorter and easier struggle to maintain and prolong concentrative power once it is developed; third, the effortless triumph of habitual practice finally making expertness a natural phenomenon. The firmness with which we hold the single idea of finding the Divine Self within and the immediacy with which we return to its quest when we become aware of having deviated from it, will mark the end of the first stage with any exercise. If the first stage of concentrated attention inwardly directed upon the mind itself is successfully achieved, the second stage will then be to prolong it. The second stage has been satisfactorily achieved when the practice is resumed with pleasure and discontinued with reluctance, when the mind is able to concentrate and withdraw inward within a minute or two of sitting down. We may arrive at such an expertness that we will be able to pass at once with ease, and at will, into the first and then the second stages of meditation.

As the effects of meditation become more and more familiar, understanding of its mechanism and facility in its practice grow with them. With the increase of facility, which time thus brings to us, the decrease of distraction will correspondingly delight us. Shorter and shorter will become the waiting preliminary period during which thoughts, memories, anticipations, emotions, and agitations aroused by our external life manifest themselves and prevent perfect concentration or delay inward self-absorption. Anyone who is already well advanced on the quest always finds the meditation time a joyous tryst with the beloved, whereas one who is taking his or her first steps often finds it an irksome meeting with boredom. The novice moves reluctantly and unwillingly to the self-commanded duty of daily meditation on the Higher Self. The proficient, who has conquered the technique, moves joyfully and eagerly to this God-blessed gift of daily communion with the Higher Self. It has passed from the stage of being a drudgery to that of being a privilege. In the fully developed meditative life there is ease, naturalness, and stability. It will demonstrate poise and show balance. The difference between a restless mind and a disciplined one is like the difference between mere chatter and good conversation.

The inner search for the Spiritual Self must go on steadily and uninterruptedly. If at first we find nothing and feel nothing, we are not to be discouraged. We are digging a well. Some have to dig far and long before water appears, therefore we should push our search deeper down. The water of life is there; we need not doubt that. Every ancient seer, every medieval saint, every contemporary mystic testifies to this fact. Our mystical progress will be characterized by an increasing withdrawal into ourselves, by a drawing back from the physical senses and an interiorizing and immobilizing of attention. Deeper and deeper will our consciousness sink away from environment and into itself. During the mind's movement back upon itself, we will quite definitely experience the sensation of going inside. It will be like trying to penetrate through layer after layer of the mind. We have to shut out not only all sensations of external objects but also of our own body's existence.

However, it is one thing to introvert attention to this deep point and another to be able to sustain the introversion itself. We must not only achieve it fully and completely, but also remain immersed in it for some time to develop its strength and effectiveness, to enable the daily renewals to become almost instantaneous. The troublesome temptation to get up and stop the effort before the full time allotted for meditation is over occasionally becomes overpowering. But to yield to it is to accept defeat. To resist it is to cut a further length of the road to victory. Or, the temptation to get up and do this or that, to think about some other matter—even a spiritual concern—will also come insistently. We must remain firm and not yield to it. This is hard to do, but only because we have for so long—for a whole lifetime probably—allowed our attention to become absorbed by the outer world that it now tends naturally to fly back there the instant our vigilance ceases. Through insistent practice and patient cultivation, we can definitely make this turning to the inner world, this silencing of body and mind, just as easy to do eventually as it is hard to do now.

We have now reached the most critical and most important part of our adventure in meditation. It is the borderline where our own effort must gradually cease and the Soul's effort must commence. We have to keep perfectly still, in body and in thought, so as to let this other presence overshadow us in a beatific quiescence. It cannot do this while we are physically busy, mentally preoccupied, emotionally attracted or repelled by something or someone. We must keep still in every way. Thus, we will introduce nothing to impede the holy presence's movement stealing over the body and taking hold of the mind. All this can be literally felt. But the slightest obstruction causes its instant withdrawal. From being positive, we must now become passive. The profound mystery of *grace* is involved here.

The psychological condition of this degree is quite involuntarily induced, whereas those of the earlier degrees cannot arise without willed endeavor. If the meditator does not brush aside its early beginnings or otherwise obstruct it, it often grows so rapidly into mesmeric

strength as to become wholly irresistible. Although it is a power outside of our ordinary self, somehow it is also a power not separate
from that self. The effect of this grace is a mighty one. With every
influx of it we feel a change coming over us, although this change
may take a variety of forms. But whatever the form, the strain that
accompanied our earlier essays in concentration comes to an end and
the struggles through which we then labored will no more vex us.
We have to feel our way into this higher mood much as the artist has
to feel his or her own way into a creative mood. Attention must here
move as vigilantly as a person walking along the narrow parapet of
an embankment that overtops a river. When the central consciousness lies effortlessly fastened to this central point, its attention now
wholly held, the period of novitiate with its disheartening failures is
definitely at an end. Our vague feelings will now begin to assume
concrete form.

If we faithfully follow these instructions and diligently perform
these exercises, we will sooner or later become conscious of this
subtle presence within our own mental atmosphere. It will be something exalted, noble, serene, and transcendental, but it will also be
something that we cannot keep and quickly lose. Nevertheless, it will
return again and again. As soon as we sit down to meditate, its spell
will seem to be magically thrown over us like the fabled enchantment of fairy tales. We should unhesitatingly surrender to its mysterious but delightful influence. The process of bringing this new life
to birth within ourselves, which was hitherto naturally a painful and
prolonged one, will henceforth be a source of growing joy. Little by
little we will forget our worldly affairs as we sit in meditation and
more and more remember our spiritual affairs. We will come to love
the calmness and contentment that these periods of fruitful contemplation bring us, which are unknown to those who despise such
exercises. The sense of satisfying rest that comes over us in this state

will always be noticeable. We will enter it each time feeling like a weary traveler who has reached the end of a long exile, like a fatigued wanderer who has returned home. During these brief periods, our consciousness will become invested with a ripeness of understanding that it does not possess outside them.

What we have most to learn at this stage is, in one sense, easy and simple. Yet in practice, it turns out to be hard and elusive. It is to "let go," to cease from striving, to let our will relax, to stop thinking that the Overself is something we must grasp and to let ourselves be grasped by it. Moreover, we are not to limit this attitude to the meditation period only, but to bring it into our ordinary life briefly several times a day. We are, indeed, to be like the swimmer who now and again turns over and floats quietly with a few gentle foot-strokes, where before we rushed noisily forward with vigorous arm-strokes; or like the archer whose task is to concentrate on drawing the arrow as far backward as he or she can attain, but not to supply the actual propulsive force. So the yogi's task is to concentrate attention inwardly as much as possible, but the actual entry into mystical consciousness is entirely beyond his or her own determining.

This inner quest during meditation is something like the outer quest of a radio listener who is twirling the tuning dial at random in an effort to establish contact with a satisfying broadcast. For meditators who have succeeded in turning attention well inward must then use it to explore their inner being in an effort to establish contact with its profoundest point, with the mystical center where everyday consciousness emerges from the Overself. Until we have trained ourselves in this mysterious art through long practice, our earlier explorations will naturally be slow, blind, and groping. But just as naturally they will be transformed with time into well-directed movements that will quickly bring us to the sought-after point. Once we touch and faithfully hold fast to it, we will have to cease being active and instead become quiescent and open to the diviner influence that will now play upon us—just as the radio listener, when having found the desired station, must remain passive and open to the sounds that will now play upon the eardrums. (We do not offer these comparisons for their exactness but for their instructiveness. They are only analogies and should not be pushed beyond their usefulness or they will land us in difficulties.)

One reason for this insistence on meditation as a part of the fourfold quest may now become clear. In all worldly affairs we are ordinarily using our personal will, whereas the philosophic ideal calls for its surrender to a higher will. The advanced phase of meditation enables us to practice this surrender in the deepest way. Hence, meditation is vastly important and imperatively necessary to the seeker for this reason alone. What we achieve temporarily in displacing the ego and stilling the mind during its short practice, will become a root from which the possibility of a more durable result can grow through the earth of our whole character.

A return to the attitude of prayer is helpful here to attract the onset of the state of quiescence. This is the way of utter humility, for it merely sets up a quest and then waits for the divinity in us to rise up and end the quest by its own self-revelation. It is a way consonant with the words of Christ, satisfying the condition that he laid down when he said, "Except ye become as little children, ye cannot enter the kingdom of heaven." The keynote of this new stage is surrender, utter and complete. We must let the divine current flow unhindered and unregulated, not attempt arbitrarily to divert it into ego-chosen channels, or it will disappear. The moment when we feel the "Overself's spell" laid upon us is a crucial one. We must submit to it without resistance and without delay. Otherwise, it may be "gone with the wind" for that day. All we have to do is to receive humbly rather than to strive egoistically. Our work is to yield ourselves up; the Overself's is to take possession of us.

If the first stage of this adventure involves an eager, willed endeavor of the mind, the final one involves a quiet, passive surrender of it. If the one depends wholly on the aspirant's own exertions, the other depends wholly on the Overself's bestowal of grace. In both the first and second stages, that is, in concentration and meditation, the will is eager and active so that the results are its own productions; but the very contrary is the case in contemplation, which is the third stage. We have absolutely nothing to do except be content and receive what the Higher Self graciously bestows upon us.

The state of attentive absorption is not a passive one. How could it be when the mind must be made strong enough to endure the strain and steady enough to hold the stillness perfectly when the thoughts are dropped? It is definitely and energetically positive to the external world, although necessarily plastic and sensitive to the influx from the deeper mind. Indeed, we must beware of making our meditation merely negative and nothing more. We must disdain the glib easy assurance so often made by half-baked mystics or incompetent teachers that all we need to do is sit down and wait passively for the "spirit" to enter into us. For this is a way that may not bring the "spirit" at all, but instead may lead either to waste of time or to psychic danger. We must not be vague, hazy, or purposeless when we sit down, should not seek a mere blankness.

On the contrary, we must be fully alert and wholly attentive, positive in attitude and definite in understanding of what we are trying to do. There must be a definite subject for our thoughts to start with and only afterward an object in repressing those thoughts. Only then may we become receptive and expectant; but such relaxation should be like that of an eagle vigilantly poised in mid-air over a possible prey below. The dangers of faulty meditation—the lack of personal instructions and common experience to draw on, which confronts the modern Westerner who attempts it; the excesses, extravagances, absurdities, and aberrations into which neurotic meditators may easily fall—all this constitutes a case for informed vigilance and common-sense controls, not at all for dispensing with meditation altogether.

What will be the physical condition of the meditator when this degree is reached?

It may be said in a real and definite sense that during the advanced stages of this endeavor, when we begin to sink in the heart and stop thinking on the way, we quite literally go inside ourselves. As attention deepens, meditation passes into contemplation and the world of the five senses recedes. We will sit like a rooted tree. For as this great stillness settles on the mind, a corresponding motionlessness settles on the body. The whole muscular system becomes unresistingly inert, every limb gently rigid. Some power other than our own captures our body and its limbs, our mind and its thoughts. We can neither stir the one nor direct the other. We are its helpless victim. For a short time the body will be powerless to move, the mouth unable to speak, and the will unable to assert itself. We will naturally fear the unfamiliar; we will instinctively recoil from entering this stage, with its apparent menace of losing consciousness or of becoming the helpless victim of unknown forces. But this condition will be a perfectly harmless one, the rigidity purely fleeting, the captivity utterly delightful. Ah! what a heavenly rapture permeates our feelings! No earthly counterpart could ever parallel it. We may even slide unwittingly into the deepest state of self absorption, when the skin on the face quite often becomes pale and tightly stretched, thus producing the ethereal appearance associated with the saints.

Whether or not our eyes will be shut depends partly on the nature of our preceding meditation exercise and partly on the special kind of grace that is being vouchsafed for the time being. Generally speaking, the indrawing process is helped by their closure, the stabilizing process by their opening. This point will not be for us to settle, however, but for the Higher Self. If they remain open, the eyes merely look unseeingly at their surroundings or into space. For the meditator's attention will be elsewhere, forgetting this world to remember a better one. During this semiconscious and automatic fixation of the gaze, the lids may gently open a little wider than normal, so that both pupil and iris are fully exposed, or else they may narrow down into almond-shaped slits. The environmental thoughtform may vanish altogether if the eyes are closed, or it may continue to exist in a vague blurred little-noticed image if they are slightly open. If the first condition arises, then there are no perceptions of the world as a field of experience and no willing of acts. In this full self-absorption, the senses cease all activity and are quite unable to take any impressions from outside the body.

But absolute withdrawal from all sense-impressions of the outward world is rarely attained nowadays by the average meditator. Nor is this really necessary. Meditators need not lose their awareness of the things around them and need not utterly forget their personal identities, that is, they need not fall into a trance of utter insensibility. Such an expectation pertains only to the ancient yoga methods, not to the philosophic path that is here expounded. The disadvantages of those old ways is that they lead to the loss of all sense-perceptions, hence to unconsciousness of the external surroundings. Indeed, pushed to their farthest point as in the yoga of body control, they lead to total unconsciousness. The advantage of the methods here advocated is that the consciousness of the world, sensations of sight, touch, hearing, and so on, may be retained to some extent without disruption of the higher condition. The trance condition is not at all indispensable to this path. It is a physical repercussion that manifests itself in some individuals but not in all.

If the consciousness is able to become perfectly concentrated and perfectly introverted, then the presence or absence of trance is unimportant. Those whose meditation attains utter self-absorption may or may not experience an entire loss of external consciousness and of the capacity to observe what is happening around them. It is not an essential condition. Indeed, modern people in a Western setting are unlikely to experience it. For them, the world does not become utterly absent and they keep throughout a hazy notion of what is going on around them. But it does become faint and far-off. They enter a profound absorption into themselves.

It happens in some cases, but not in all, that on reaching what is called the "neutral" point of our meditation, which is the point where our consciousness of outside things suddenly transforms itself into consciousness of the fundamental Self, we will slip insensibly into a total lapse of consciousness, which will be exactly like a refreshing deep sleep. But this is not likely to last longer than a few moments or minutes.

Whatever physical end is the outcome of our successful adventure in meditation, we will invariably find that, for a brief while, we will seem to be without a body—a fleshless entity of pure thought, an invisible spirit of passive calm. It is after such an experience that we may come to feel that the body is an alien self.

If physical sensations and environmental images are more or less banished from the mind by this interiorizing of attention, abstract ideas, felt emotions, or pictured forms, which have been deliberately set up as an object of concentration, become substituted for them. Now these, too, must be banished from the mind. Just as the attention has already emptied itself of sense-reports, so the intellect now slowly empties itself of thoughts and the imagination of pictures. This is the last important sign to occur when the second stage ends. The passage to the third degree is almost unwittingly and insensibly effected. The reasoning process is silenced, the memory fades, the image-making faculty ceases to operate, and a mystical quietude descends.

When the state of reverie can be induced without being a reverie on anything in particular, when we are able to stop all movements of the mind, when we are able to hold attention steady without fixing it on any object or thought in particular except our own spiritual being, when we have learned the art of being still, when we can cease running after thoughts, and when we stop trying to keep step with time, we have learned this part of the exercise.

First, thinking must dismiss its objects; next, it must dismiss its own activity. For in this final stage, intellect impedes contemplation. We must initiate this process but we cannot consummate it; this will be brought about by a force outside our own volition. We may try forcibly to repress all thoughts, to arrest all intellectual operations and all emotional movements, but success will come only when and if the Higher Self takes a hand in the game. We may, however, greatly assist the process by understanding what is required of us in the various stages by the light of knowledge that has here been furnished, and by offering no resistance through fear or ignorance to the unfamiliar and mysterious changes within our psyche, which the Higher Self seeks to bring us.

The power that grips our mind will not let it form any thoughts, or, if it succeeds in doing so, will not let it hold them. That which clears all thoughts out of our consciousness is nothing less than grace. We reach a point in our inward-bound journey when we are inhibited, and the faculty of reasoning ceases to function. Although there is a complete silencing of our thoughts, there yet remains the thought of the concept or symbol that represents the higher power for us and receives our devotion and aspiration. But it is a thought held, fixed, immovable, not leading off into a train of succeeding ones. Our attention must be so finely concentrated on that "other"—whether it be our Higher Self, our idea of God, a revered scriptural personage, or a living spiritual guide—that in the end we become absorbed in it and pass away from the knowledge of our own personal existence. Now we must let even this last thought go altogether and then hold fast to the sacred emptiness, sacred because an indescribable sense of divine beatitude overwhelms us. When this final thought-activity gently, almost insensibly, comes to an end, with it the centering of our consciousness in the personal individuality also necessarily ceases. But this does not mean that all consciousness ceases. Instead, it shifts over to our higher individuality, our Soul. Consciousness, in the ordinary form that it takes with the present-day person, will go, but it will not be lost.

This is the psychological condition of "giving up self" to which every spiritual teacher has pointed as being of climacteric importance. There will be an overwhelming sense of release and then the ego will be taken up into and absorbed by the Overself. We feel that another self has emerged from the mysterious deeps of our own being and taken hold of us. What takes place is a veritable displacement of the lower consciousness by the higher one, just as the volume of the water in a vessel is displaced by an object that is placed inside it. We have effected a passage from the lower self to the higher, from the lower will to the higher will. It is the sacred moment when we actualize our higher potentiality, that is, when we become conscious of our divine part. "By not thinking nor desiring, she arrives at the mystical silence wherein God speaks with the soul, teaches it wisdom," explained Miguel de Molinos, Spanish adept who was martyred for his services to mystical seekers throughout Europe.

Although it is said that the Overself sits waiting in the heart, only now can we understand why it would be a mistake to consider it as a merely passive entity and the way to it as a one-sided endeavor. On the contrary, it has guided our search and draws us inward to itself and sheds its quickening grace at various times. Only now can we perceive that what we believed would be our own final discovery is, in reality, a veritable act of self-revelation on its part, just as the final act of union is a self-absorption by it. If in the first stage the mind must leave outward distractions and in the second leave inward ones, in this third stage it must leave its own egoism. The search for the inner reality of our own selfhood, the quintessence of our own consciousness, has come to an end.

Although we feel ourselves drawn into another world of being, we also feel such life-giving self-completion in this experience that we know with absolute conviction that it is what we have always most sought and most valued. Indeed, while we are in this state and wholly gathered in it, we experience the extraordinary feeling that we are no stranger, that we have always been here and that it is our natural condition. In this deep slumber of the body's senses and the person's thoughts, the primal mode of our real being is found. We know then that this is the infinite source of our finite existence. Here tired wanderers rejoice at last in return to their true native land. The conviction that this, indeed, is the Real will be more intense than we have ever felt before with other kinds of experience. That there, in this mysterious region, the Higher Self has through long ages awaited us and that this meeting with it is the most momentous of our whole life, is an intuition that flashes poignantly through us.

At such times, it is the Soul that takes control of the everyday self. A definite feeling that we are mounting up to a higher level of our being, a joyous sense of liberation from the ordinary vibrations and customary agitations of the ego, naturally accompanies this psychological state. This makes us feel complete and satisfied in ourselves, a wonderful feeling that we will never better. The Self we now realize is as superior to the ordinary ever-frustrated ego as are real flowers to the artificial variety. In this moment when the contemplative mood fully matures, we feel that we have passed over from a lesser into a new and higher dimension of being, that it is a state whose reality and authority certify themselves, that it is mentally illuminative, that it throws our personal wills into abeyance, and that nothing we have previously desired can be so satisfying as this desireless consciousness.

In the happy iridescence, the majestic silence, and the dynamic awakening of this experience, what has heretofore been a mere mental concept, an ineffectual bloodless notion, the *Soul*, now becomes filled with life and power. The personal ego's normal control vanishes, but its own consciousness is not suspended while the Overself's pervades us. The two exist side by side, like two concentric circles, one inside the other, but with this difference: for the time of this overshadowing, all the evil in the ego is entirely neutralized, all worldly attitudes and earthly desires are utterly transcended. The whole moral nature is sublimely elevated. The current that entered into us acts as a solvent upon the last remnants of our lower nature. It seeks especially and stills immediately the animal desires, the intellectual doubts, ill-will, pride, inertia, and restlessness.

With the fading out of sensations, thoughts, desires, emotions, and volitions in the deepest stage, the ego and its earthly interests fade out altogether. When all the faculties have gathered themselves into the mystical quiet, when will and thought lie passive in its still embrace, when no thoughts enter to disturb it, the mind is naturally even and serene to an extraordinary extent. The stream of ideas comes to an end. We sink in a blessed quietude—wide, deep, and complete—never before known. As we approach nearer and nearer to the Overself, we become more and more conscious of the stillness that appears to surround it like an aura. The passage in meditation from ordinary consciousness to mystical awareness is a passage from corrosive turmoil to healing tranquillity. We seem to enter a land of eternal rest and silence, whose mysterious peace spins an incredible enchantment. A curious feeling of being laid under a benign spell comes over us. It is as though a little circle of impassive stillness has been drawn around our seated figure.

There is a dead silence, which is merely the absence of words and there is a living silence, which is really the presence of divinity. It is about this condition that St. Augustine in Europe counseled, "When thou inwardly hearest the affirmation 'Truth,' there remain if thou canst." And it is about this same condition that Gaudapada in the Himalayas advised, "Touch it [the mind] not when it has found the condition of evenness."

But if meditators must not let themselves fall away too soon from this inner stillness, on the other hand they must not allow the habit of remaining overlong in it to grow. It has already been mentioned that for this practice at the contemplative degree twenty-six minutes will suffice. Such counsel is given only to students of philosophical mysticism, however, for it is only they who seek a balanced integral attainment. It will be rejected by all others, so it is not tendered to them.

Sometimes the shedding of the grace, which draws the consciousness "inside," is so swift in its operation that it has forcibly to overcome the ego's resistance. When this happens, there is an abrupt but intense focusing of emotion upon the heart, a sudden but overwhelming yearning for the Soul that dwells within it, and a tremendous agitation of the thoughts generally. The eyes may close involuntarily, the better to concentrate, with muscles around and behind them drawing tensely together around a common center—the gap between the eyebrows. After a while the nervous excitement subsides and a beautiful calm replaces it. Then there will arise the loving, joyous perception of the Soul already described.

The meditator who reaches this state—and it is only a determined few who do so—enjoys its enthralling condition for a limited time only. There is a repeated experience of being possessed by the Overself for a brief while, coinciding with an occultation of the ego, and then the reappearance of the ego coinciding with an occultation of the Overself. This sense of being overshadowed by another being, enclosed and held within its divine aura, presently stops. Unheedful of our desire, the visitation comes to an end. Neither by power of will nor by cunning of thought can we prevent this loss from happening. Such a profound self-absorption is not attainable for more than a short time. To be granted this blessed period is one thing; to be able to sustain it is quite another. Nevertheless, if the beautiful experience passes, its beautiful memory remains. A hallowed light rests upon these shining hours.

THE INTEGRAL PATH

If it be asked why these states are not sustained outside the peak hours of meditation, the answer lies concealed with the question itself. *Meditation alone is not enough.* The fulfillment of all the conditions regarding meditation exercise will advance us in our vocation as a mystic, but will not be sufficient by itself. What is still required of us is that we should become *philosophical* mystics, should unfold the possibilities of our whole psyche and not only our intuitive ones. The effort to attain spiritual awareness is not only a matter of the acquisition of concentration; it is also a matter affecting every side of our life. If the quest were only a technical process and its problems only problems in meditational technique, it would be easy enough. But it is much more than that. For it also involves the emotions, the desires, the will, and even an unknown factor—the Overself's grace. An integral and total quest must be followed. If, for instance, the aspirant meets with blockages when attempting to go inside in inward-pressing concentration, it is certain that some of those blockages arise from earthly attachments and extroverting desires. Hence, an analytic purification of the heart, an emotional pruning of it, is indispensable side-by-side with efforts to achieve the one-pointed, stilled mind.

We can make a success of meditation only if we have veneration and sensitivity, only if we give it the character of an act of tender devotion and make it bear the quality of heartfelt reverence. The failure to obtain successful results is, in a number of cases, due entirely to neglect of this rule. It is an indispensable condition of progress in this quest that love of the Divine Soul should become ardent and fervent. Only the complete fourfold path can lead to a durable realization. Therefore, our further efforts are to be directed toward this end. It is this joint effort of will and intuition, of thought and feeling, which constitutes the integral path. By steadfast practice of meditation and by assiduous efforts along these other lines, we become able in time to transfer at will to this deeper state and to sustain consciousness therein. When, through the united and elevated efforts of thinking, feeling, willing, intuiting, and aspiring, this meditation upon the Overself as being our own self becomes serenely uninterrupted and permanently stabilized, it can be said that we have attained life's highest goal.

TWO

Is the Soul
in the Heart?

THIS QUESTION IS REALLY an ancient one. Centuries ago the Indian thinker Silanka sarcastically complained in his *Sutra Kritanga Tika* that "Some posit a soul that has a form while others maintain that it is formless. Some point out that the heart is the seat of the immortal Self, while others oppose them by saying the forehead is the right place. How can there be an agreement of views among these philosophers? For us ignorance is far better than these follies."

The master key to the comprehension of this difficult point is taken hold of when we grasp the notion of two standpoints and consequently discriminate between two levels of existence: the one apparently real and the other absolutely real, the one a transient appearance and the other an eternal substratum of this appearance.

Thus this apparent anomaly can be explained; thus and thus only can views so opposed be reconciled. The Overself that I have written about in earlier books represents the esoteric notion of it. Even so, I pointed out the paradox of its being both inside the human heart, simultaneously with its unbounded existence outside the human body. Such statements are perfectly correct from the standpoint of ordinary yogic existence because they describe the actual feelings of the mystic.

However, I did not frankly give the full ultimate truth about the Overself being entirely outside all considerations of spatial location. That is because I was following an ancient principle of tuition used by Asiatic teachers, one in which truth is adapted to the capacities of different minds, and knowledge unfolded only partially and progressively.

It is like the difference between gazing at an unopened nut for the first time in one's life and gazing at it when unhusked with the kernel lying revealed. At first we see the husk but believe we are seeing the nut; later we see the real nut and only then know that our discovery of the husk was but a stage—yet a necessary stage—toward our discovery of the kernel.

Spiritual *feeling* does center itself in the mid-sternal region of the chest. As practical people we must experientially affirm that the Overself has its habitat in the heart. But as metaphysical people we must flatly deny the existence of any special point wherein it could be cramped. Only the sage who has mastered philosophy, who has harmoniously perfected ego-less action yoga and metaphysics, can afford to dismiss all sectional viewpoints; others must attend to them or else unbalance their progress. When meditation succeeds in attaining its objective, yogis do have a definite experience of bliss, a joy of liberation from Matter and ego. Such an experience transcends any that they have ever had before and is so exalted that they believe they have entered into union with the Overself. Indeed they have really achieved their goal, but it is only as seen from an earlier standpoint, like a mountain seen from far off. They have approached immeasurably nearer to the realization of the Overself than ordinary religionists with their remote anthropomorphic God, for they have found

Deity within themselves. Nevertheless it is still not the ultimate real-ization. They have yet to pass through the metaphysical discipline and the ultramystic contemplations before this union is finally con-summated in the discovery of the Overself as it is in itself, not as seen from any standpoint. With this discovery, they are delivered from the need of further meditation because the Overself is then found anywhere—not merely in the heart alone. And this is not a transient experience but a permanent insight.

The mystic view of the matter is not inconsistent and need not be negated; it can be kept where it belongs and yet be included in and harmonized with the higher philosophic view. For no prac-tical yoga system can be devised that does not in its earlier stages demand some focus for concentrating the thoughts. And in placing that focus within the heart region, the mystic follows the best means of withdrawing attention from external surroundings. Hence the Svetasvatara Upanishad says: "Placing the body in a straight posture, with the chest, throat, and head held erect, making the senses and the mind enter the heart, the knowing one should cross over all the fearful currents."

The Mundaka Upanishad also counsels: "Just in the heart, where all the blood-vessels meet, very much like the spokes of a wheel meet-ing in the navel or the center, resides the interiorly-governing Divine Spirit, manifesting His glory in ways multifarious. Contemplate Him, this interiorly-governing spirit, for, thus alone can you reach, with safety, the blissful haven, far beyond the ignorance-begotten miseries of this troubled ocean of life." The Gita XVIII, 6, says the region around the heart is the divine center. "He has set eternity in their hearts," says the biblical Ecclesiastes. "The Heart is the greatest, the most primal cavity Residence of the Self; the body of bones and flesh is Its temple. Those who study this Secret Path realize that the individual is that Self and nothing else. The five senses, which are robbing an aspirant of his robust Self, are the candles to exhibit the Inner Light," wrote Tirumoolar, a Tamil mystic of the seventeenth century.

It is an indisputable fact that although visions of divine figures or the light of the Overself are clairvoyantly *seen* in the head, the presence of what is most divine *in* us is mystically *felt* in the heart, for Nature herself has made a mysterious and holy vacuum therein. The Overself as such is formless, but its *manifestation* within the heart possesses form. In the unimaginably minute airless space within the heart where this manifestation abides throughout the whole length of an incarnation, there appears a picture formed of light, a picture that outlines the precise prototype of physical body of the person concerned. In our measure it is but a fraction of a fraction of a dot in size. Yet it is there. This is the "little person within the heart" of whom Tibetan occultism speaks, the "figure in the heart" space of Indian mystical Upanishads. In my earlier book, *The Quest of the Overself,* it was explained that the divine habitat within the heart was not a thing but a space, symbolically called a "cave" by the ancients and in reality a kind of vacuum.

The authoritative Pali* commentators on Buddhist texts expounded that the mind or consciousness is dependent on the heart-base, although the Buddha himself never stated the organ in which it existed. They must have had their reasons for doing so. One school of Vedanta teaches that Brahma's abode in us is in our vital center, in the smallest ventricle of the heart. On the other hand, some yoga teachers place it variously in the top, center, or base of the head. Shankara, the sage and commentator, reconciles these seemingly contradictory teachings about the seat of the Spiritual Self. He shows that in deep sleep the different places are entered in gradual succession. This does

---

*The Buddha's original teachings were recorded in India in the Pali language.

not mean that each has the same purpose or importance. Shankara points out that they fulfill different ends. Thus the spirit occupies the heart at one point of time and the head at another.

The actual place in the physical body where awareness of the Soul seems to come to birth differs according to the particular exercise in meditation deliberately practiced, or according to the particular kind of mystical experience involuntarily and spontaneously received.

It is a fact, however, that in most cases the feeling of the Soul's presence is first felt in the heart or breast region. But if the mystic should pass into a deep meditation akin to half-trance, as the feeling deepens and strengthens itself, it also spreads itself out into the Infinite. It is then no longer limited to the heart or the head, in whichever place it first made itself felt.

It is a tenet of the hidden teaching that Mind has two phases: conscious and the unconscious, or active and the inactive. The second is the root and determinant of the first phase. And it is a further tenet of this teaching that the conscious mind is correlated with the brain. Science can find corresponding changes in the brain for every change in sensation, that is, in consciousness; but science cannot find any such physical change in the brain for the principle of awareness itself, that is, for the unconscious. If it were to direct its researches in this regard toward the heart, its efforts might hope for better chance of success, because it is there only that the corresponding bodily changes could ever take place. But as the principle of awareness is an unchanging one, no physical changes ever correspond to it in actuality. It is ever present during life. It is like a circle whose circumference is the entire body and whose center is the heart. A shot through the heart is fatal not only in a physical but also in a mental sense.

What is achieved during odd illumined moments, however, is not enough, for these moments are at first but intermittent. The process of descending into the heart must be rendered habitual; our central consciousness must be transferred from the brain to the heart. This does not mean to say that we are to become incapable of thought; only that thought will assume a secondary and subordinate importance in our life, and that the supreme place will be given to a focused attention upon and enjoyment of the peace within the Divine Atom* resident in the heart. We may then use the brain at will and think no less clearly, no less efficiently, than we formerly did; only we will no longer become the hapless victim of thought's tyranny.

When we still the active intellect, we feel the pressure in the head relax and a feeling of peace begins to suffuse the heart. This is also a physical feeling, so that there is really a descent from the busy intellectual region of the head to the quiet spiritual region of the heart. Mystics rest their consciousness in the heart habitually, except when they have to enter intellectual activity for a time.

We descend from meditation in the brain to meditating in the breast. Such a statement may be incomprehensible to those whose thoughts and meditations have forever revolved within the sphere of cold ratiocination alone, but it will make some sense to the few who have begun to feel the first and almost impalpable radiations of the divinity that the heart harbors. For our real home is in the heart, not the head. We have strayed afar.

---

*For additional information on the heart atom, see *The Quest of the Overself.*

THREE

The Interior Word

If thou would'st hear the Nameless and wilt dive
Into the Temple-cave of thine own self,
There brooding by the central altar, thou
May'st haply learn the Nameless hath a voice.

Tennyson, *The Ancient Sage*

When he, the Spirit of truth, is come, he shall guide you
into all truth: for he shall not speak from himself; but
whatsoever he shall hear, that shall he speak.

Jesus

Which things also we speak, not in the words which
man's wisdom teacheth, but which the Holy Spirit
teacheth.

St. Paul

If thou can'st do what He enjoins on thee, He will do
what thou dost ask assuredly.

Awhadi, medieval Persian mystic

A STRIKING MYSTICAL phenomenon is the "living word" as some have called it. This is the interior communication through clearly framed messages from the Overself. It is a form of speech where every sentence is endowed with magic, where every word is a vital force, and where definite effects flow from each communication. It works in and on the heart and sheds wisdom's light on the mind.

All inspired bibles are the records of this inner utterance. They are the echoes of this same speech, but drained of its life-giving power, its supernal, over-worldly tone, and its vivid authority. All true gospels are spoken in this mystical inner language, are heard only in the heart and not with the ears, are creative transfiguring forces and not mere intellectual statements. What is heard within the heart is indeed the Logos, the Divine Word, which can be heard only in this way. That which is written or printed on paper can be no more than the word of humankind, not God.

This mysterious power of the deep silence within ourselves to break into speech will at first astonish and then delight. If we persevere in our practice, the silence within will little by little take voice and guide our further efforts. Its words may reveal divine truths, afford spiritual guidance, or explain the inner significance of situations and events. Negatively, it will reprove our sins, warn us of our errors, and humiliate our egoism. Positively, it will lead us to higher standpoints, show us the right path to follow, and illuminate the true meaning of all scriptures. It will correct our attitudes, direct our behavior, and instruct our mind. And we who have attained to the hearing of this inner voice will always be glad and willing to obey such commands. We must learn to listen to the inner voice and heed the inner light rather than the teachings and guidance of others. It will come to possess an indisputable authority and a supreme truth. But it can do so only after we have learned to distinguish it clearly from its rivals and enemies—only with time, experience, and constant self-examination.

After we have won through to the stabilization of this experience of the inner voice, we will find an inward teacher perpetually within our heart. Henceforth the Higher Self will impart knowledge steadily to us, either in the midst of activity through *intuitions* or in the depths of self-absorptions through *inspirations*.

By this method we will be taught continuously and instructed progressively. We will be led by a voice speaking in our hearts, from stage to stage, truth to truth, and perception to perception.

It is a mysterious voice that breaks the silence of ignorance that reigns in others and every word of which is creative, dynamic, and loving. The voice that now speaks perpetually is no metaphorical one. It is so real that even once heard it is more unforgettable than any human voice—however beautiful—could be. It is so sacred that we receive its utterances with the reverence accorded to scripture, for they are nothing less.

When inward converse with the Higher Self develops, the ego vividly feels the presence of its Beloved and expresses its longings and prayers, its joys and reverence. Through the Interior Word the Soul responds. These interior conversations may become a feature of our lives for a certain time, the ego addressing its Higher Self on some occasions, the Higher Self addressing the ego on others. We may often have the strange experience of participating in dialogues between the familiar ego and what seems to be a higher one. That we are receiving communications from the Divine may well be a genuine fact. But the form they take is inevitably imposed on them and colored by our own personalities.

And I make it my business only to persevere in His Holy presence, wherein I keep myself by a simple attention, and a general fond regard to God, which I may call an actual presence of God; or to speak better, an habitual

silent and secret conversation of the soul with God,
which often causes in me joys and raptures inwardly.

BROTHER LAWRENCE, SEVENTEENTH-CENTURY
MYSTIC, *PRACTICE OF THE PRESENCE OF GOD*
(TRANSLATED FROM THE FRENCH)

That we need only to recognize God intimately present
with us to address ourselves to Him every moment,
that we may beg His assistance for knowing His will in
things doubtful, and for rightly performing these, which
we plainly see he requires of us, offering them to Him
before we do them, and giving Him thanks when we
have done.

BROTHER LAWRENCE, *PRACTICE OF*
THE PRESENCE OF GOD

The dialogues may develop spontaneously, and it will be a useful exercise to cultivate silent conversations with the sacred presence
whenever the slightest tremor of its nearness is felt. Dialogue often
concerns revelations, guidance, counsel, encouragement, and the
answering of questions. There are fine specimens of this form in the
third part of *The Imitation of Christ*.

A kindred phenomenon to the Interior Word is the dialogue
between some higher being, often regarded as God or as an angel,
and the mystic. He or she will receive the words but will not see
their speaker. For the Interior Word is a different phenomenon from
that where some spiritual personage of the past or present appears in
vision. The first is more reliable than and always to be preferred to
the second. This is because it is a communication to the mind alone,
whereas the other is also a communication to the senses, which, being
on a lower level than its source, are far less fit to judge it. The mystic
is aware of another presence, a holy entity, somewhere within, and

a beautiful fellowship with it gradually develops. It speaks to him or her within the mind, and not to bodily ears, so distinctly and so spontaneously that he or she cannot doubt its real existence. This mysterious entity within the heart has life but not shape, voice but not face.

Once we truly awaken to the god who sits concealed in our inmost heart, once we have learned how to enter the silence and pass through it, then out of the interior silence there will sound forth the Interior Word. This amazing moment when the silence of the Higher Self is dramatically broken, when its voice speaks in our hearts, will repeat itself at intervals, first in our periods of withdrawal for prayer and meditation, then at any time. This is the mystic voice heard by Samuel and by all inspired prophets. "Speak Lord, for thy servant heareth," was Muhammad's response to it. It will bring healing to our nerves and bear its own authority to our minds. Authoritative messages may thus be received from this Higher Self, formulated in distinct words but without any sound. During sessions of mental quiet the Overself may reach the ego in either a wordless or word-ful way. A presence is felt, an inner voice is heard, an uplifting ideal is presented. Some have called this striking mystical phenomenon "the living word." Speech forms itself in the mystic's heart, he or she knows not how, and communicates revelations or gives counsel. What I have elsewhere called intuition, which more than anything else is a feeling inside us, is not the same as this, which is more like someone speaking to us. It is an aspect of the Overself's power.

The mysterious inner voice, which utters no sound that the ears could hear yet formulates messages and communicates guidance of spiritual importance, arises within during trance. These communications will, however, refer only to the inner life. They will give no guidance for the outer life.

We should listen intently to the silence that we will find deep within our heart, deeper than all the passions, emotions, instincts, desires, attractions, and repulsions that usually pulsate tumultuously there. No one else can do this for us. The voice that will presently make itself faintly felt will seem like a messenger from another world. Something or someone will begin to stir in our inner being and address itself to us. Wise and instructive, warning or inspiring, this mental voice will seem to be another's. Yet, later, we will become aware that it is not so, that it is, indeed, the voice of our own best mind.

Although the experience may not be in store for everyone, it is possible that some aspirants who are sufficiently advanced may find themselves gradually entering into a heritage of great powers, which have awaited them since the dim evolutionary past and which have slowly germinated deep down within their being during all these mystical efforts. The first of these mystical powers is to hear the Voice of the Silence.

It is needful to learn the art of distinguishing between the true and the pseudo Interior Word. If it manifests itself during the second stage and before the aspirant has ever been able to touch the third stage, it most probably is the pseudo-word. It may then be a result of mental activity on the ego's part mixed with a little reflected light from the Overself. The true word comes after the third stage. It speaks out of the mental stillness of contemplation, and is indeed one of its striking effects. It is the Voice of the Silence.

"I will hearken what the Lord God will speak in me." Psalm 85 testifies to the truth of this same experience. Similar testimony is found in Asian scripture.

Dr. Singh has translated the *Gorakh Bodh*, a dialogue between Gorakhnath and his teacher, Matsyendranath, which bears comparison in style and importance to the yoga Upanishads. An extract follows:

QUESTION: Who can tread a path without feet? Who can see without eyes? Who can hear without ears? Who can speak without words?

ANSWER: Contemplation can tread without feet; discrimination can see without eyes; attention can hear without ears; the self-born can speak without words.

Eternal wordless truth is brought into time and expressed in space.

FOUR

Self-Reliance or Discipleship?

How many questionable visions have been suggested to meditators by their so-called spiritual guides? How many mystical experiences would never have occurred if this guide had not said to expect them? How much near-mesmeric phenomena masquerades as mystical experience? Consider those who are so fascinated by the ancient tenets and methods that they surrender themselves wholly to them and live in the past, wasting precious time relearning lessons that they had already learned in those former epochs. They are victimized by the dead. They ignore the lessons of Western civilization. Why were they reborn in the West if not to learn new lessons? Should they not be sufficiently flexible to adapt themselves to the demands made by the present era? Uninspired, unenlightened teachers who do not perceive this continue to teach the old methods alone, phonographically handing down what they have received by tradition. If they could realize the vivid inner spirit of their inheritance rather than its musty outer form, they would become free of the past. For then they would stand alone in the great Aloneness. And out of such a spirit they would instinctively give what is needed today, not what was needed by former centuries.

The disciple who places himself abjectly under the thumb of a supposed master, or turns even a good person into the object of a superstitious idolatry, becomes a mere robot. Those who have not the courage to think, speak, and act independently of their teachers will never have the chance to realize truth for themselves. Those who overweight the value of a master's services to their disciples are ruled by emotion, not reason, when they study no other system than the one promulgated by their masters. When, in short, they have completely surrendered themselves in every way to the master, then it is right to say that they will never know truth, never attain realization, never become sages themselves. The slavish mentality that so-called teachers and pseudo-gurus create and perpetuate in their unfortunate disciples leads to their moral degeneration. Losing faith in their ability to attain truth by their own efforts, they do not try and consequently attain nothing.

As soon as people yield up their souls in blind belief to any dictatorial exploiting guide, the light of conscience goes out and the voice of common sense is stilled—they begin to walk in darkness; they cannot see whither they are being dragged. Those who follow such a teacher will in the end, if they are fortunate and sincere, be driven by disappointment to the necessity of retracing their steps. Those who surrender themselves wholly and blindly to him or her, surrender the very opportunity for which they have taken birth in a human body. The teachers who hand them a readymade teaching, which they have nothing more to do than to believe, block their real path of progress and hinder their true development. Thus, instead of making their enslaved disciples conscious of their inner resources and awakening their inner power, these teachers put a wholly exaggerated valuation on their own service and try to make students forget their self-reliance altogether. They become more weak-willed and more negative than they were before.

The priest played a dominant part in former epochs and assumed on his own shoulders the burden of truth-seeking. But his work misdirected itself when it brought people to believe that without the mediation of others, without the intercession of salaried sacerdotal hierarchies, it would be impossible for them to achieve a spiritual status. It is unfortunately an historic fact that in ancient and medieval times especially, almost every priesthood tended to arrogate to itself social, political, and economic privileges upon the alleged sanction of its title to deputies for God on earth. Exploiting these privileges came in time to occupy the minds of many priests more than the advancement of humanity. It is not genuine religion but selfish priest craft that, in the name of God, has so harmed and hindered human progress. This is why we see that an important part of the mission of such great souls as Jesus, Buddha, and Muhammad was to curb the unhealthy power and erase the superstition-fostering influence of the orthodox priests of their times.

It was always easy enough for the credulous, uneducated, underprivileged masses to fall victim to the promises and threats of priest craft, but a parallel if more refined system of exploitation developed where it might be least expected. It appeared in a different stratum where it tried to hold its grip through the medium of exaggerated guru-worship on those who had evolved beyond the orthodox religious state into mysticism. The spiritual teacher originally represented one who gave guidance and assistance to the seeker, but misguided belief came in time to make him or her represent God incarnate to the seeker. In the East particularly, the ignorant deification of living men and women with the consequent slavish obedience and renunciation of intellect that this often entailed, once went and still goes to the most fantastic lengths. It has fostered widespread superstition, despoiled self-reliance, and destroyed independent thinking. It has opened easy gates to many charlatans.

The custom of getting people to regard some other human as the incarnation of God may have been helpful in ancient times when the masses were simpler-minded than they are today, but has decidedly led to unfortunate results in modern times. At best, its value was on the practical and not philosophic side, to the untutored masses and not to the cultured classes. To ask modern votaries of mysticism to follow the same custom is to give an unhealthy direction to their inner life and a misleading one to their intellectual life.

When guides, who are still frail and fallible because they are still human, are taken as divinity, when they are credulously draped in deific titles and reverentially enshrined by their disciples far beyond the profane reach of common reason, the philosophically minded can do nothing else than gently smile and silently withdraw. To be worshipped by others is, in their view, not a privilege but a nuisance. To call any guru by the Deity's name and to ascribe deific power to him is sheer blasphemy. The truth about this has been plainly and tersely set down by St. Paul: "I have planted, Apollo's watered, but God gave the growth" (1 Cor. 3:6).

Philosophy is devoted to teaching principles, not to aggrandizing, glorifying, or exploiting personalities. It holds that the authority of the messengers is not of such primary importance as the truth of the message, that priority belongs to what is permanent and not to what is transient, and that people need a reorientation of thought and renovation of practice much more than reverence for particular individuals. It worships divine ideals, not human idols. It substitutes the veneration of verities for the adoration of persons. It declares that whoever persists in worshipping dead persons, like Jesus, is throwing thoughts into the vanishing void, but that whoever worships the immortal principles *taught by Jesus* is laying up treasure in heaven. It seeks to inculcate great truths rather than to idolize great humans. It is not concerned with what A or B has said or done so much as with whether A or B's words are true and his or her deeds right.

Let us entertain no illusions about this matter. Let us indulge in no wishful thinking and thus unwittingly deceive ourselves or unjustly deform truth.

We have often heard in recent times of this or that nation wishing to establish its political independence. We do not often hear of this or that person wishing to establish his or her mental independence. Yet such individualization of the human being, which is the present evolutionary goal, cannot be reached without it. That which was accomplished in former centuries by an appeal to blind faith must now be accomplished by an appeal to scientific rationality. No one and no group has a prescriptive right to own another person's or another group's mind forever. No teachers of today are ethical who prevent their students from discovering and developing their own latent and inexhaustible resources, however permissible it was in primitive times. The belief that there must, however, be somebody to walk beside us all the time, to guide our thoughts and acts continually, a leader to whom we must always be looking up, is not a belief that philosophy can entertain.

Within the very broad limits of faithfulness to the path, the teachers should allow plenty of freedom to students to choose their own steps upon it, to develop along their own personal lines, and should encourage them to think and feel as free individuals.

All the religions of the past sought to enfold humanity within groups; the tribal or racial outlook still clung to them. This was right under the external conditions that previously governed our social existence. Only a thousand years ago the inhabitants of America, for example, were completely cut off from those of Europe. Consequently, the religion useful to the one people was not useful to the other; their habits and heredity were quite different. But today these conditions have been astonishingly changed. The planet's face has been transformed by human handicraft. Humans have now the possibility and power to think universally, to choose for themselves the ideas they want to accept and the ideals they want to follow. We are becoming mentally individualized. We can begin to reassess the values of life and the ideas of existence, not as mere units in a tribal or national group but as self-respecting individuals. This, indeed, is simply democracy at work in religion. But in taking this step, we have taken the first step toward mysticism. For mysticism itself is the culmination of all sincere religion. Some instructive details about the second evolutionary movement may be found in the ninth and tenth chapters of *The Wisdom of the Overself.*

THE WAY OF ORGANIZED GROUPS

What has here been said of personal leaders and individual teachers applies equally to authoritarian, hierarchical institutions, and public or secret dogma-bound organizations. Stereotyped religio-mystical institutionalism is forever suspicious of members who would seek for truth with free and independent minds. If they persevere in the search, sooner or later they are sure to collide with it. When that happens, and they find it neither politic to compromise nor wise to submit, they will be thrown out as rebels, excommunicated as heretics.

When we perceive how frequently these organizations have become the traditional enemies of their followers' inner progress—as in the cases of Buddha and Jesus—prudent seekers will keep away from them, giving them their good wishes rather than their memberly presence. When they learn from biography and history how inevitably formal bodies tend to drive out what is most important and manage to keep what is least important, they will learn how dangerous gregariousness is to truth.

Most organizational forms are too illiberal and are committed by their very nature to the maintenance of past narrowness. They quickly become new cages for aspirants to enter. Religionists are now such tight-bound prisoners in the structure they have erected that they may not utter these truths even if they know them, whereas the philosopher is now so impressed by the dangers that confront humankind that he or she must utter them.

If students of philosophy are to join any group, it should not be an external one. It should be bound together by no visible ties but only by a common mental austerity of attitude, a common devotion to the quest for truth. They should not wear labels and cannot bear organizations. For the one would separate them instantly from every other spiritual group and the other would force them to entertain thoughts of rivalry and struggle for worldly prestige or power at the expense of competing organizations. It is one of the beauties of philosophy that it is the only worldview that seeks no proselytes, makes no propaganda, and possesses no vested interests. It is the only one that grants a true and total freedom; all others thrust their followers into cages.

People admire a popular movement largely because it is so large. They worship brazen idols while dust collects on the golden ones. It is unlikely that a teaching that sets itself the most exacting standards will have a popular appeal. Philosophy is cheerfully prepared for that handicap. It clearly sees that it is intended for the discriminating few and its sphere of operation inevitably provides it with well-defined limitations. It cannot hope to affect or awaken the multitude immediately and directly, hence does not seek to win their favor. Therefore the fact that its followers may be no more than a mere handful will not disturb the peace of its custodians. If they can become an instrument of esoteric enlightenment and individual regeneration for these men and women, if they in their turn can thus be inspired to serve others in their own way, it shall surely be enough. They do not strive for the suffrages of the masses. The success they aim at does not consist in the larger number, the great recognition, the wide approbation; it consists in reaching the waiting few who are ready to listen, to appreciate, and to understand.

Philosophy is encircled by a little audience of devoted followers and will not be so unwise as to stray beyond it. It has deliberately sought to limit its field of influence. It wants the friendship of its followers but it does not want this on a false basis. If pleasing their prejudices, catering to their sentiments, confirming their wrong notions, and supporting their illusions are to constitute this basis and not the quest for truth, then such friendship would not be authentic. Rather than concern as to whether or not people are prepared to listen, it is a duty to place before those who seek it— and to make accessible to them—the highest counsel and the wisest guidance it is able to give. Philosophy is an educational and not a propagandist movement. Therefore, it does not seek to compete with any other for the simple reason that it cannot. It is forced to restrict itself to the few whose interest in its special teaching is deep and devoted, whose minds are sufficiently ripened to be naturally sympathetic toward it.

It may now be better understood why there is no sense of disparagement in our statement that philosophy is set apart from the motley crowd of other teachings by reason of its uniqueness. That is merely a matter of character-making destiny. The others have their place, but not one will be able to fill that of philosophy. It must be boldly emphasized that it breaks exclusive ground in reflection about, and penetration into, life. Once *understood,* even by a handful of competent persons, this knowledge makes its own way in the world. Its dissemination is not to be secured by noise and shouting but by understanding and living it. These are the reasons why it modestly voices its subtle message and does not play the part of a raucous loud-speaking propagandist, why it exemplifies in its calmness and dignity its own injunction on how to meet the ups and downs of contemporary events. It will not shout with the crowd but always pursues its own policy.

Advanced aspirants are bad "joiners." Philosophy is sufficient for them. They will never again feel the need to adopt a new faith or follow a new leader. They are not eager to follow their flightier sisters and brethren every few years into the latest cult. They will always show a prudent reserve toward new prophets and coteries, teachers and doctrines, and refuse to commit themselves to them headlong. They will not agree to shut their minds and quests in a closed system. They will not accept anything that restricts their views and narrows their perspectives. Hence, they will not, for the sake of their own spiritual advancement, join any sect or organization, any institutional religion or mystical cult. People who are captured by philosophic truth are captured forever, for it has set them free. Once a philosopher always a philosopher. We shall never hear of them dropping their allegiance to philosophy. If such a hitherto unheard-of event ever did happen, it would be only because the renegades had never really accepted true philosophy. For it alone deals with reality, not with fluctuating emotionalist feelings or intellectualist opinions about reality. Once we have dug our way to the rock-bottom foundations of the higher teachings' architectural structure, be sure that we will never desert it but will become more loyal to it with every year that passes. Yet it would be foolish to expect that more than a microscopic minority—those born with a burning desire to understand the innermost significance of life—will ever take the trouble to dig so deeply. Therefore, only a few of those who merely *read about* it will ever be completely loyal to it.

Throughout its long history humankind may be conveniently divided into these two groups: those who consciously dedicate themselves to the search after truth, and those who do not. The quest is only for someone who is willing and able to step out of the herd, for the sufferer who has had enough of blind living, and for the thinker who is more attracted by the lonely path of an austere individualism than by the over-trodden road of a self-deceptive orthodoxy.

How many promising souls have had their integrity violated and have been forced to abandon the path along which intuition was correctly leading them to lofty attainment, only to be placed by their organization, group, or personal guide upon a path that led in the end to disillusionment or disaster. Those who attach themselves to teachers share not only their "wisdom" but also their ignorance and errors. Such a possibility might not have mattered much in ancient times when teachers who had *realized* truth could be found without excessive difficulty, but it matters greatly in modern times when one may comb an entire continent and fail to find such a one.

THE WAY OF DISCIPLESHIP

There are many aspirants in the West who have spent the best and longest part of their lives in the expectation of meeting, or in the search for, a spiritual guide of the rank of a mahatma or an adept. They have done so because Theosophy—especially Neo-theosophy of the post-Blavatsky period—and Indian Vedanta have told them that the initiation, assistance, and continuous guidance of such an exalted personage is absolutely indispensable to the spiritual quest, and that without initiation the quest can only end in failure. But their search has usually been a vain one.

Now we fully admit, and do not deny, the assistance that may be had from a true teacher. But a trustworthy guide through the dark maze of mysticism is not easily found today. Where some believe that they have found such a master, quite often their search has been worse than vain—for it has also been self-deluded. They actually endanger their inner life when they join it to a dubious inspiration and an undue subservience. We are here not passing judgment but merely stating facts. The difficulty of finding competent, pure, authentic, and unselfish instruction is today so great, and only a little less so in the East than in the West, that it seems to us wiser to emphasize publicly the possibilities of making progress by a self-effort, of unfolding latent resources without overanxiously seeking here and there to obtain a teacher. For so many aspirants are wasting precious time and energy in futile search and disappointing experiment, when they could be making progress and reaching maturity by availing themselves of their own inner guidance.

When we mention this rarity of qualified reliable teachers, the retort is often made that the mystical tradition contains a saying, "When the pupil is ready, the master appears." We would not contradict the truth of this saying, but we would complement it with another truth—that the master here referred to is not necessarily an embodied or an external one. He or she may be out of the flesh or may be inside the pupil's own heart. In both these cases the instruction will come and assistance be rendered from within through the intuitive faculty. Or the master may be a printed book left for the guidance of posterity by one who had successfully finished the quest. There are many excellent books obtainable nowadays in which most aspirants can find sufficient reliable instruction to suit their immediate practical purpose. But in the end, that which brings together the seekers and the sought-for truth, whether the latter be found within themselves, a book, or another person, is the direct agency of their own Overself.

Owing to suggestions implanted from without, the heart's yearning for the Spirit is easily mistaken by beginners as a yearning for a master. Those who are mesmerized by past traditions—especially Eastern ones—or misled by present cults into accepting the suggestion that it is impossible to advance without a guide, merely transfer to the search for a human being what should be a search for their own Soul. In their ignorance they superimpose his or her name upon it and honor another with the worship that should be given to the Soul alone. Instead of setting out in quest of their own Soul, they set out in quest of a human. The one being within themselves and the other without, the directions are totally opposite. Consequently, the two quests must lead to two different results.

When the Christ Self, speaking through Jesus, said, "I am the door," it gave counsel which is still fresh today. It meant "Do not look for other people's doors; do not turn to other people for that which your own Higher Self is waiting to give you." The solemn proclamation of this Christ Self in each person is: "I am the Way, the Truth, and the Life." In ourselves we can find the guidance needed, the knowledge desired, and the goal sought. But to do this we must have full faith in the Christ Soul within us and not go wandering from one person to another. Either this Soul exists within us or it does not. If it does, it is necessarily a living and active force behind the scenes of our visible life. It is surely as competent to guide us on the spiritual path as any embodied human being. If it is not true that our own Soul can directly guide us, that it can by itself lead us into self-realization, then there is no truth in the claim that it exists nor in the records of its power. But the fact is that the voice that is calling us is the Soul's, even though we ignorantly give it someone else's name. If this quest is nothing less than a search for our own deepest self, then the clinging to another human self, to external masters, can only prevent and not promote attainment.

Just as the seeker has to learn through disappointment and suffering to cast off sole dependence on any human being for happiness, so we have to learn through the same means to cast off sole reliance on any human being for guidance. The Higher Self alone can give durable happiness and it is the Higher Self alone that can give perfect guidance. In the end we are brought back by the tragic events of life to the essential solitariness of every human soul. And it is only when we are courageous enough to face those events and this solitariness in all its fullness, looking to no embodied person for assistance, that we have the unique chance to discover our secret inhabitant, the Divine Soul. When we have come to realize through such disappointments and disillusionments that we must entrust ourselves to the guidance that comes from within, not only because it alone perceives the needs peculiar to ourselves but also because it emanates from that very second Self that we are trying to discover, we have come to the true entrance of the mystical path. We have fulfilled one of the conditions to authentic enlightenment—we have turned away from other things to the direction of the Soul itself.

If we have to pass from the elementary into the higher grades, we can do so only by awakening to this advanced truth—that our own Soul is the rightful God-given guide. When we have traveled sufficiently far to be able to understand this situation, we will start to form ourselves and not wait uselessly for some master to do it. We will begin to shape our ideas and direct our meditations for ourselves and not lie supine and helpless until we can receive them from outside. We will exercise our will and not let it lie flabby, inert, or even paralyzed.

It is the students, and the students alone, who have to crush all evil passions, reject all evil thoughts, overcome all evil emotions. For they are theirs and unless they deal with them, the weaknesses of character that gave birth to them will still remain. It is not only absurd but also self-deceptive to count on a master doing this for them. No external agency can assure them externally what they must assure for themselves internally. The knowledge that is born by their own thinking, the strength that is drawn from their own selves, the compassion that comes out of their own hearts, is immensely superior to the second-hand products of exterior suggestion. Those who act on this truth will need no one else to teach them. The Divine Self is there, ever present, and will do it better.

Even Sri Ramakrishna, the saint whom many of the swamis themselves follow, adoring him as an incarnation of God—even he has admitted, "He who can himself approach God with sincerity, earnest prayer, and deep longing, needs no guru." It also is true that the saint qualified his statement by adding, "But such deep yearning of the soul is rare; hence the necessity of a guru." If the yearning is strong enough and deep enough, it will find what it truly needs without much help from outside. But if it is not, then it may become the circle-wandering slave of a dozen narrow and unsuitable techniques, the enfeebled victim of a dozen exploiting teachers, before it becomes aware in the end that it has to find the path that conforms to its own individual characteristics, before it receives the liberating teaching that comes from the purity of its own Overself.

For each is an individual and therefore unique. To imitate always the thinking, speech, and action of a particular teacher, to accept always the suggestive influence that he seeks to exert upon mesmerized followers, to practice only the method that suits such a teacher—this is not to travel the path to the wider freedom.

Therefore, let nobody be led away into self-betrayal by the stereotyped formulae of any teacher or the mechanical laws of any technique. This does not mean that we will brusquely or foolishly reject whatever we can derive from others, but it means that while accepting such aid we will not assign it a primary place, will not make the success or failure of our quest rest unduly on it. If we understand this situation correctly, this will not mean dependence merely upon the limited resources of our personality but upon the unlimited resources of that which dwells behind the personality. We will look, in short, with unshakeable faith to the Overself to lead us finally into that realization of divinity that is our sublime goal.

"I am forced to draw my philosophy from my own head," remarked Socrates, who learned his teaching from no one. His own wisdom was dug out of the hidden depths of being. No teacher set his feet upon the path, no school transmitted it to him; it was self-obtained. Therefore, it was natural that he himself should not care to unload a pack of ready-made doctrines upon other people's shoulders but rather endeavor to bring them to self-thought. A teacher's instruction at best leads to mediate knowledge, whereas the realization of truth must be immediate. The former is necessary as a preliminary step leading to the latter, but it cannot of itself give realization. Students must therefore make their own efforts to realize what they have been taught. They cannot escape this duty if they want reality and not merely words or thoughts about it. As in Socrates' time, the seekers of today find themselves in the same position where self-effort is called for. It may be a fact that the old Sanskrit texts anticipated many of our eventual conclusions but we have to travel toward them by a different route. For we have now to walk alone with unaided thought and by pioneer experience. When we are compelled to stand on our own feet, we are compelled to study our own problems; what we thus gain is our own and cannot be lost.

After all, it is of little use looking to others to provide that which, in the end, we have to provide for ourselves. We may flee to the imagined security of a master, a method, a creed, a church, an ashram, a group, or an organization, but we flee in vain. In the end, life demands that we discover our own resources. At best, as Socrates has shrewdly pointed out, the teacher can but work like a midwife, helping students to deliver themselves of their own truths. We should understand that mostly we must work out our own salvation. All insidious suggestions intended to enhance dependence, weakness, and enslavement must be resolutely resisted by those who would be philosophic students. The first task of a true guide, therefore, is to create this necessary self-reliance within them, to help them become conscious of their own latent power, to encourage them to nurture their own understanding by recommending reflection upon their own experiences. Intellectual integrity demands this of them—that they do not wholly subordinate liberty of action to another individual, that they do not become wholly subservient to the teacher's will, and that they do not wholly forfeit their free will. If it is true that it is unethical to tyrannize over weaker people, it is equally unethical to yield to the tyranny of stronger ones.

It is the students who must liberate themselves from their own illusions, for no master can do it for them. They may momentarily and occasionally see the truth through the eyes of a master, but they cannot enduringly and unbrokenly see it through any other eyes than their own. If the master really wants to help students, the healthy way is for him or her to get them to use their own understanding independently, to give them enough confidence to develop their own powers of comprehension, and to promote their concentrative power and stimulate their thinking power. Thus, students learn to trust increasingly their own inner resources and to convert aspiration into action.

In opposition to the orthodox views selfishly held by the heads or blindly followed by the advocates of other and older Indian schools, which declared enlightenment to be quite impossible without a teacher, the Buddha plainly if heretically declared that there are two ways whereby one can arrive at right insight—either by learning it from others or by self-reflection. The same point has been differently explained in detail in *Yoga Vasishta,* an old Sanskrit text, thus: "There are two kinds of paths leading to truth's freedom. Now hearken to them. If one should without the least failure follow the path laid down by a teacher, delusion will wear away from him little by little and emancipation will result, either in the very birth of his initiation by his guru or in some succeeding birth. The other path is where the mind, being slightly fortified with a stainless spontaneous knowledge, ceaselessly meditates upon it; and then there alights true enlightenment in it, like a fruit falling from above unexpectedly." This second path is the one we have advocated. It is based on rationally thinking over and mystically meditating upon the remembrance of a glimpse, intuition, or fleeting illumination that may have once been experienced or, alternatively, upon the description of such an experience as given in books.

There is a plain inference to be drawn from these facts. It is that—students who are thrown back upon themselves by the statement that the Overself is the one true teacher to be sought above all others—nobody has really been hurt. In depriving them of doubtful external guidance, we have given them back the surest internal guidance—the light and power of God within their own selves. We have endeavored to awaken them, to bring them out of slavish dependence on others, to lift them up from being weak leaners to becoming self-reliant learners, to arouse them into the consciousness of their own powers of achievement and their own possibilities of knowledge. We have tried to help them to look at life from their own spiritual center and draw out of themselves a wise comprehension of life, and to work by the light of their own creative ideas rather than by borrowed ones. We have sought to help individuals develop into the awareness of their own inherent divinity and thus fulfill the true purpose of their incarnation. The only redemption that philosophy proclaims is self-redemption. It believes that we must create out of our own consciousnesses and by our own efforts the new understanding that shall transform us. For, in the end, realization of the Overself is nothing else than a shift of emphasis within us and, therefore, no outside force can effect it.

"Hold fast as a refuge to the truth. Look not for a refuge to anyone besides yourselves," exclaimed the dying Buddha to his attendant disciple Ananda, when giving a parting message for all disciples. What he further said is also very instructive with regard to our subject. "Be ye lights unto yourselves" is one acceptable translation, but "Be ye islands to yourselves" is another. Whether we accept the one or the other, the meaning in both cases is ultimately the same. It is a message of self-reliance, of seeking within and not without for guidance and strength. It is, finally, a warning not to depend unduly on human teachers but mostly on the illuminative element within oneself. "Work out your own salvation with diligence," were the last words of this wonderful man, whose reposed form, smiling mouth, and peaceful countenance evidenced his own sublime self-reliance.

THE CHOICE BEFORE THE SEEKER

Nevertheless, only the unbalanced extremist can wish to dispense with wise instruction of the right kind, if it be available. For without it we must experience trials and must make many mistakes and suffer much in consequence, too. Yes, the need of a reliable master is great. But such a one must be not only a person of knowledge but also of power and pity—power, because those who come to the quest are so weak themselves, and pity, because there is no other inducement for him or her to help them. So if aspirants are incapable of working out their hard problems by themselves, they should seek and accept the guidance of someone else. To obtain friendly guidance from someone who knows the farther stretches of the road is as sensible a procedure as it is senseless to become the debilitated mental slave of someone who exudes pontifical infallibility and discourages scientific rationality. It is the primary function of a competent teacher to show a sure, safe road to pupils and thus shorten the effort needed, as it is his or her secondary function to impart a propulsive impulse toward the goal.

Most aspirants find that the Overself is not a thing they can aspire toward or meditate upon so long as it remains inconceivable, unimaginable, and ungraspable, by their ordinary mind. It is a formless, characterless, and featureless void with no point of reference for them. It is too intangible, too vague, and too indefinite for their consciousness to feel elevated by or for their attention to become concentrated upon. They are left by this concept suspended in mid-air, as it were. Their need, therefore, is for something or someone to provide a visible focus for aspiration toward reality, an imaginable center for meditation upon it. That is to say, they need an attractive symbol of the Real.

They can find such a symbol in a historic scriptural personality known to them by tradition; in a living master known to them by personal acquaintance; in a book, ancient or modern, whose sentences purport to be inspired by the knowledge of reality; in the musical, pictorial, sculptural, and other artistic productions of human genius; or in the beauty, grandeur, immensity, and serenity of Nature herself. A few flowers resting in a simple vase may also convey, to some refined mentalities, an adequate symbol of divine graciousness. But whatever it is, it is indispensable that it should appeal to their personal predilections if it is to become effective. Even the accessories, instruments, ceremonies, rites, and sacraments of religion can also be utilized for the same purposes, provided this condition is fulfilled, and provided they are regarded, not in the light of the extravagant claims usually made on their behalf, but as tokens of the intangible and as reminders of the quest. The statuette of a Buddha plunged in contemplation can thus become fraught with significance in the eyes of Buddhist mystics every time they behold it, both as a hopeful message from the silence of nirvana to desire-bound persons and as a stimulant to the further practice of meditational exercises. The little crucifix carried underneath a shirt may become alive with meaning to the mind of the Christian mystic every time it is touched, both as a sign of the presence of the hidden spirit "crucified" in a manifested universe and as a remembrance of the need of dying to the lower ego.

The aspirants who have found a trustworthy contemporary guide, an ideal teacher who has united with his or her own Soul and is willing to help others seeking to attain the same state, may conveniently regard such a one as their finite symbol of the infinite Overself. To accept this person as a spiritual guide will not then be a blunder. On the contrary, it will be an act of wisdom, for it will help them greatly to go forward. It will give the mind something definite with which to occupy its field of attention, something that can be not only taken hold of by both thought and feeling during the aspirational hour, but also retained by them outside it. Hence, for those who have not reached the stage of fully operative mysticism—which is not an easily reached stage because it is such an advanced one—it would be foolish to underrate the value of such external helps, unwise to lack appreciation of the usefulness of such a symbol.

There are certain other advantages, over the more impersonal kinds, of utilizing a master's name and person as a focus for this kind of meditation. It is easier for many people to work imaginatively with the familiar physical senses than creatively with the much less-used faculties of abstract reflection. For we can quickly create the mental image, can rapidly remember the sense of elevation yielded by the impact of the master's aura; can set up an activity wherein greater strength to concentrate and apter skill to turn inward are drawn telepathically from this living presence; and can thus find a visible object for pent-up feelings of devotion, an object to whose likeness we can try to conform our own strivings. During such meditation, there will be a satisfying feeling that there is no longer a compulsory confinement to the aspirant's own limited resources.

"When the pupil is ready, the master appears." But this need not mean a physical appearance; it really means a mental appearance. When pupils are to some extent purified and self-disciplined by their own efforts, rendered more sensitive by meditation and instructed by study, then the Overself may direct their thoughts to some developed person as a focus for their further meditations, prayers, and aspirations. We say "may" here because this does not always happen. It depends on the individual's history, circumstances, inclination, capacity, and character. Spiritual ties created in former births may be so strong as to necessitate a teacher-disciple relation again for a time. The need for a devotional outlet of a personal and tangible character may be so overwhelming as to make it imperative to find a worthy one in order to facilitate further progress. The natural weakness of most human beings may foster depressive moods that paralyze endeavor, so that encouragements and stimulants from stronger human beings become needful.

On the other hand, we may have cultivated self-reliance, independence, and balance to such an extent that we are untroubled by all these considerations. In that case, no master need or will appear. Our own Overself will provide direct guidance from within instead of from without as in the above cases.

Where we are brought by our own wish and fate's design into touch with a master, even then it is not necessary that we stay permanently with him or her. It is enough to be with the master for a few minutes. But even if we have not met the master, the establishment of contact internally through correspondence is sufficient. And even if we have never corresponded with the master, the absorption of thought from a book he or she has written will lead to some result of this kind.

To imagine that we actually are the saint who is our ideal, to picture *ourselves* as being suddenly transformed into the guru we follow, is indeed the shortest and the quickest method of *mystical* attainment. But it is given to a disciple only toward the end of his or her adventures in meditation. For one has to be sufficiently purified in character, expert in concentration and contemplation, metaphysical in separating formless being from its external appearance and detachable from the personal ego, to be able first, to use such an effectual method and second, to use it in safety and without incurring harm.

In this exercise we must act the teacher, pretend we are him or her, and call up all histrionic ability to imitate the teacher's ways. The initial acceleration of our lapse into contemplation will begin when we think of the teacher's form in this way, but the final consummation of it will come when we unite with the teacher's essence, his or her mind alone.

When imaging the teacher, we should think mostly of the Spirit that is using the teacher's body. It is more effective—and hence the more advanced part of this exercise—to think of him or her as a medium for the higher power, as a vehicle for the divine presence, than merely as a self-sufficient person. It is not of the flesh-and-blood guide that we are to think so much as of the mind that is inspiring the guide. It is not personality in its ordinary state that we are to imagine but in its extraordinary state of absorption. We are to contemplate and identify with the guide's inner consciousness when plunged in the same deep meditation that we seek to attain. We are not to worship the person but rather the Spirit that has taken possession of the person. We are not to concentrate thought on the fleshly frame so much as on the presence within it. It is not the name of the dead prophet or living guide that is to receive our homage and devotion, reverence and prayer, but rather the nameless being that overshadows the person. Thus we pass from appearance to reality; thus we prepare to become a vehicle of the same divine life.

It is the ideal represented that is to be worshipped, not the person. We should venerate his or her embodiment of the ideal, of the heart and mind in a perfect condition. Philosophy ardently advocates the necessity of veneration but does not advocate a blind and credulous veneration devoid of wisdom. We should venerate the master not because we want to turn a human into God, as the superstitious often do, but because we want to turn ourselves into a master, as the philosophic try to do.

There are many stories that seem to show that even if they have not given enduring realization, many gurus have at least given transforming occult experiences to their disciples. What is the hidden truth about this matter? Where these experiences occur in the teacher's presence and lead to a state of half or full inward absorption, they are of a hypnotic character. If teachers are really of a superior kind and have really gone deeper into their own Souls than ordinary people, they will be able to communicate something of this depth to students if the latter fall into such a self-absorbed state. It is very useful, in its own place, for a student to taste what the next stage in mystical meditation is like. From the philosophic standpoint its value is limited because of its transient nature, because the psychic revelations that often accompany it may be merely hypnotic suggestions of a dubious kind, because it cannot yield permanent results, and because students will still have to work out their own development to this stage. The character and worth of such experiences have often been grossly exaggerated in India, in ignorance of the historic fact that the annals of Western mesmerism record many cases of similar experiences where the mesmerizer was not necessarily a spiritual person at all.

Where, however, disciples experience the psychic presence of a teacher, although they are in different cities or widely separated lands, when under such conditions they perceive the vision of a teacher's face and form confronting them, and when they hold daily thought conversations with this living presence and form, it is natural that they should come to the conclusion that the teacher is actually with them in some "astral" body and that the meetings have been deliberately willed by the teacher and successfully brought about by his or her yogic power. But these conclusions may be erroneous. The facts on which they are based may exist only in the student's imagination. The teacher will most probably be quite oblivious of what has happened to the student and quite unconscious of these daily visitations and telepathic conversations.

What has really happened then? The answer is that the form taken by the student's experiences and the ideas it yielded were entirely self-suggested. The student's own concentration on the idea of the teacher, the tremendous faith in the power of the teacher, the great devotion toward the teacher, have unlocked the latent capacities of his or her own mind and turned them temporarily into kinetic forces. Thus, instead of disproving the existence of yogic powers, this interpretation of these experiences actually proves it. Only it is not the teacher's but the student's powers that are really in question.

This explains most cases but not all. Where the teacher is a person of genuine Overself-consciousness, a further force is brought into play. There is a spontaneous reaction to the student's thought about the teacher, but this comes from the Overself direct to the student and over the head, as it were, of the teacher. It is, moreover, not necessary for the adept to think of each disciple separately and individually. It is enough if he or she retires daily from contact with the world for a half hour or hour and turns attention toward the Divine alone and opens as a gate through which it shall pass for the enlightenment of others. During that same period, all those who are mentally devoted to him or her will then automatically receive the transmitted impulse without their even being consciously in the adept's mind at the time. But such a guide is rare and such cases are consequently exceptional.

Disciples of such a qualified master who live at a far-off distance, or in a foreign land, and are consequently able to meet only at long intervals if at all, may nevertheless benefit by the mystical link that exists between them. If we have developed sufficient sensitivity through meditation practice, we will feel at critical times, or after periods of intellectual perplexity, that we are mentally in the presence of the absent master and either receiving spiritual help or conversing with him or her upon the subject about which enlightenment is needed. In this way, our drooping spirits may be revived and silent questions answered satisfactorily through a genuine telepathic process. The impact of such a teacher's power on the disciple's mind cannot but be beneficial.

Therefore, a fifteen-hundred-year-old Chinese text, the *Chisto Tao Lun,* says that a beginner on this quest should search and inquire for a person who possesses insight. If we are unable to find such a master, then we should search and inquire for one who is well versed in meditation and well advanced in knowledge. Having found a suitable teacher—even if younger than ourselves—we should, the text continues, respectfully express our desire for enlightenment and assistance.

The help that can be given by such a guide is to be admitted, but, because there are few philosophers in the world and comparatively many more mystics and metaphysicians, the difficulty of finding it unentangled must also be admitted. For they may have made some mystical or metaphysical progress and be willing to assist others to do so too, yet their attainment may not be sufficiently perfect to free them from adulterating this willingness with other motives. They may be swayed by the desire for financial gain, by an unconscious yielding to the sex impulse, by the wish to exercise power in the world, by the complex of being worshipped by many followers, or by unseen powers that are tempting them to their own destruction. Progressing mystics, betrayed by their own ambition or spurred by their own arrogance, may take to the teaching path before fit to do so. One result is that they become exploiters, not teachers. They dominate the souls of their disciples, deliberately prevent them from finding out for themselves anything that is hostile to the teacher's interests or doctrines, issue arbitrary orders and expect unthinking obedience, hinder and do not help the true growth. When they want their students to slavishly echo all their teachings under pain of denunciation as heretics if they do not, when they ritually treat every manifestation of independent thought as sin—then they do not really teach them. They merely extend their egotism to include their students, enlarge their "I" to overflow into them.

It is not difficult to find such a guru possessed of mixed motives or of the desire to exploit others, who simultaneously possesses the desire to enlighten them. Where the instrument is itself impure, the inspiring power cannot but be equally impure. It will be an intermittent shuttling between the Overself at some times, and the egoistic illusion at other times, with bewildering results for the unfortunate disciples, for they cannot be expected to understand what is happening behind the scenes of their guru's mentality. We say "unfortunate," for they may be led aright on some points but will surely be misled on others. It is most desirable, therefore, that if seekers feel they must find a guide, they should find one who is personally in such a position that they need not be affected by these temptations. That is to say, they should be karmically fortunate as well as spiritually competent—either they should have independent financial means of their own or should have achieved financial success through the exercise of a profession or business; they should be happily married; they should possess, through the accident of birth, a respected position in the world or have attained it through professional, business, or social services. These, of course, constitute ideal surface qualifications but it is next to impossible to find them all combined in one person. Nevertheless, it is well to know them and, hence, to seek for someone with as many of them as possible.

The ancient ideal of a completely ascetic teacher who had entirely renounced the world cannot externally exist in modern Western civilization today, outside of sectarian monasteries, but it can exist internally in the heart of a person who has absolutely mastered his or her thoughts and emotions, even though he or she does wear the best clothes. Five hundred and fifty years have passed away since Shaikh Sharfuddin, a Sufi sage, wrote a letter in Persian, which contained this clarification for a seeker: "A spiritual teacher is not the body, the head, or the beard visible to man. He is, in reality, the inner being in the region of Truth." The wisdom of these words is needed today and will always be needed. Aspirants should not be influenced by the slave mentality of monkish teachers who will regard with shivering horror the picture of a modern guide such as we have here pointed out, but should use their God-given capacity to think for themselves and comprehend that the form under which instruction is imparted must adapt itself to the needs and conditions of the times if it is to be genuinely useful.

An honest teacher must be something more than a benevolent onlooker. Such sincere, genuine spiritual guidance as seeks to make the aspirant eventually able to dispense with the services of a guide altogether is healthy and helpful; but such selfish, bogus, or incompetent guidance as depletes the aspirant's own powers and intelligence is unhealthy and harmful. The first places a key in our hands and bids us use it, whereas the second neither possesses a key nor, possessing, would be willing to give it away. Instead of increasing students' feelings of weakness, the true teacher endeavors to instill in them the heightened confidence and deeper conviction that come with the personal exercise of their own powers. For the teacher's ever-present aim is to lead aspirants toward attaining their own proper maturity. While the right kind of teacher, like the right kind of book, will not save students from doing their own thinking, he or she will certainly help them to do it well. The teacher cannot pursue the quest for them, but can help them to pursue it in the right direction. The right kind of teacher must be able to convince pupils of the truth of their teaching—not all at once, of course, but within a reasonable time. For muddled thinking and vague perception, insufficient experience and incomplete development inevitably disclose themselves in dark obscure expression and imperfect unconvincing exposition.

I sometimes think of the ancient wisdom as a giant statue, magnificent and beautiful to behold when it was made, but now, alas, fallen into the desert sand, half-buried, prostrate, slowly crumbling, waiting perhaps for some Napoleon of insight to arise one day and lift it. I sometimes even play with the thought that the disincarnate voice of a custodian of this half-lost wisdom may suddenly issue forth from the world's radio sets and speak those authentic words that many students would so gladly welcome. For is it not the sages' business to preserve the teachings of the philosophy of truth, to keep them from fading out of humanity's memory, and to guide people into the ways of realizing the Overself in their own experience?

But alas, it is no use being befooled, whether by others or by one-self. The fact remains that *sages,* in the old integral sense of the term, are now a vanished race. Let us not waste our time looking for such perfect people. We are unlikely to find them. Let us not expect to meet gods walking upon this earth. Let us not ask where such sages exist and where they can be found. Who is there who knows? All that has been written on the subject is really a composite picture of different advanced types to be encountered and of the ideal master of whom to dream. So, let us take good guidance wherever we get it and be glad that we do receive it, whether from someone who has gone some way or from an inspired text written by a sage himself or herself, whether ancient, modern, Eastern, or Western.

This situation being what it is, students must keep a clear sense of the realities that compose it. If historic change has largely brought about the disappearance of teaching sages and thus hindered the opportunities for the progress of present-day aspirants, it has also brought about the appearance of new opportunities that have helped it. In two points, at least, they are better off than earlier seekers. They have available today the written or printed memorials of the thoughts and conclusions, the labors and victories, the methods and results of a host of seekers, yogis, mystics, sages, and philosophers who lived in different centuries and in different lands throughout the whole world. The knowledge developed during some thousands of years can now be added to their own store. If a guide is most valuable for beginners to chalk out their path, to advise them in perplexity, to explain difficult doctrines, and to protect them against pitfalls and snares, it is equally true that such guidance can also be obtained from available books. They have also available easier living conditions, which free them from the absorbing manual toil and drudgery that swallowed up so much of the effort and energy of those earlier people.

THE INDEPENDENT PATH

In the end, seekers arrive—and must arrive if they are going to advance at all—at a stage where they must learn to walk by themselves, must learn to extract from within all that is needful. Students who walk alone may make some mistakes, but they will also gain useful experience and develop their own responsibility. They will become learners instead of remaining leaners. And, in the end, another person can only teach us what we need to know and do, but cannot set us free from the ego, from the limitations of the consciousness evolved to its present point throughout so many ages of evolution. The belief that true teaching can come only from outside is an erroneous one. Indeed, sooner or later it becomes essential for us to learn the loftiest kind of self-reliance, that wherein we will look more and more to the Overself for guidance, and nowhere else.

It is true that were we to adopt a wholly independent attitude prematurely—that is to say, before we were ready for it—we would commit a grave error; but when we reach the study of philosophy, the ripe and right moment to begin to adopt it has arrived. Thus, the paradox arises that just as the stage of long search for a guide is itself overpassed when a guide is found, so the stage of discipleship must, in its own turn, be overpassed if the Overself is to be found. The embodied master must be given up for the disembodied Overself. Just as the developing mind grows out of the belief in an external and personal God, replacing it by the belief in an inward and impersonal God, so little by little it grows out of dependence on an external and personal teacher and replaces it by dependence on the inward impersonal Soul. The disciple can now see that all means—from elementary ceremonial rites, the following of scriptural injunctions, and the study of metaphysical or mystical books, up to personal discipleship itself—have been merely temporary and successive pointers to the real means, which is to renounce everything and everyone else for an utter surrender to the Overself alone. They were needful and helpful in spiritual childhood because they could be seen, touched, and read, because they existed as sense-perceptible forms in space and time. But because the Overself exists in the invisible, intangible, nameless, timeless, and spaceless Void, those who seek it must at last step out of such sensual limitations and seek it there alone in all its pure transcendence.

Only after we cease to search for any human teacher, because the usefulness of such a search has been exhausted, do we begin to receive the inner counsel, which shows why all enfleshed teachers have to drop out of our lives. Persevering seekers learn, in short, that they must surrender the false independence of their little isolated finite life, not to this person or that one, but to the indwelling ever-present universal being within their hearts; that there is no use going any longer to human beings; the last step is to go directly to the Ultimate Mind itself. The grace we need and seek must come from God. No institution can grant it. Any claim to the contrary is merely an act of human exploitation, not an affirmation of divine instrumentality.

This explains why no divine human ever appoints a direct successor. That usually occurs only in the institutions that arise around or after him or her. Whenever this has happened, the successor is invariably not up to the stature of the predecessor. In fact, the degeneration of all spiritual institutions is due to the belief that historical succession is really possible as an inward and authentic fact rather than as a merely outward and apparent one. Spiritual genius is individual and unique. It can no more be delegated by such external methods as spoken or written appointment than artistic genius can be delegated. Shakespeare could not by such an easy method appoint a successor capable of writing plays as perfect as his own. Indeed, if this were really possible, divine men like Jesus and Buddha would have saved all humankind by the simple process of transforming everyone overnight. Humankind would have been immensely superior and gloriously different from what it now sadly is. But they did not do so because they could not do so. The work that they did was good but always unfinished. The condition of spiritual genius must be attained by diligent effort and protracted striving through many a lifetime. No gurus can abruptly give away their higher consciousness as a permanent gift, though they can and do give temporary glimpses of it. No gurus can lastingly effect an enchantment wherein a disciple's entire past evolution and present characteristics can disappear entirely and abruptly.

In the superstitious adherence to the doctrines of pontifical, apostolic, episcopal, hierarchical, and lamaic succession, often with an accompanying pretense of infallibility that arises out of this single error, we may discover the genesis and evolution of most religious imposture, degeneration, hypocrisy, and materialism. All such doctrines are philosophically untenable and intellectually unhealthy. The only true line of valid succession is that every avatar predicts, before passing away, the coming of the next avatar. Thus his or her words give hope to those who, living later and in a period of degeneration, become concerned about the future of humankind, just as they guarantee to others that the World Mind will not forget its mortal progeny.

Now I can look back, with a better balance and a surer judgment than ever before, upon a varied life of more than thirty years' spiritual seeking through service, aspiration, meditation, reflection, study, travel, and personal contacts with holy men, if anyone were to ask from what source I derived the greatest help and made the quickest and farthest progress, I would be forced to answer—in contradiction to traditional Indian belief in this matter—that it was not from the holy people but my own manifold striving and humble prayer.

Indeed, I would add the further conclusion that the importance attached to persons in both religion and mysticism is nearly always a most exaggerated one. It arises out of the human weakness that regards the formal symbol as more attractive than the formless spirit, the tortuous allegory more convincing than the clean-cut concept, and the sensuous image more real than the abstract idea. Yet it is the teaching that always outlives the prophet—the truth that is the essence of its messenger and the principle that is above the personality. This is why, in my published writings, I have tried to lead seekers away from mere personalities to sublime principles.

Nothing in the foregoing pages should be taken to mean that I am opposed to organizations and institutions as such. I recognize that they have a proper purpose, which is to conserve spiritual gains and prevent spiritual teachings or literature from being lost. If they have the right people at the top, if they are worthily conducted, if they are vigilant against falling into the vices of exploitation, selfishness, and materialism, if they sincerely keep always in view the inner purpose of their coming into being—then, indeed, they may play a useful, helping, and honorable part. But if they are turned into machines for dominating minds, tyrannizing consciences, serving private interests, and conserving superstitions—then I am opposed to them.

Those who have so far followed me with adequate understanding will now understand also that I have made no attack on the institution of discipleship itself. I have tried only to reveal its proper function and mark out its proper limits.

The physically blind person will not hesitate to ask for and obey the leading of a guide. The spiritually blind, however, do not even do this much, for they suffer from delusions and imagine that they are seeing their way when they are doing nothing of the kind. Although the Buddha taught spiritual self-reliance, opposed priest craft, and exposed guruship, he did this only because he found himself in a land where these things had been so abused and pushed to such extremes that they did more evil than good. The Buddha did not intend his teachings on these points to be universally held and eternally valid. No sage ever adopts such an attitude exclusively. The sage is always practical and therefore always gives out what will best help the period and place. Only students, by their own experience in trying this and testing that, can develop the capacity to solve their own problems, can ripen the power to discriminate between the real and the apparent, the true and the false, the good and the evil. It is indispensable to our progress that we discover our weaknesses, errors, and ignorance, and then seek to correct them. But this is not to say that we must always experiment blindly and move from one mistake to another. We can utilize the knowledge of those who, in the past, have gone before us on the road of life and of others who, in the present, have gone ahead of us on the same road. Anyone can reach the highest goal by his or her own power—that is perfectly true. But if we have a teacher to remove our doubts and correct our errors, to strengthen our capacity for meditation, inspire our efforts, and explain our duties, we will reach it more quickly and safely. There are times when everyone feels the need for something or someone to rest on, to whom one can appeal for help, encouragement, instruction, inspiration, and direction, to assist through the dark corridors of hopelessness and doubt. Certainly, it is common sense to look for the guide who can provide these things. Without being too cautious on the one hand or too rash on the other, we may seek a teacher. It is only by such an ideal balance that our efforts will achieve the best result possible under given conditions.

But it is hard to find such a person, hard to find the ones who unite in themselves wisdom, compassion, experience, strength, and the willingness to serve others without reward. The average seeker will have to look long and warily before finding a competent or even an honest guide. What, then, are we to do? Shall we be so foolish as to entrust ourselves to an incompetent, a dishonest, or an insane teacher? If we refuse to do so, and are too discriminating to accept a sham substitute, are we to fall deeper into depression, sink more and more into despair? Or shall we trust the plain words of Jesus: "Seek and ye shall find. Knock and it shall be opened unto you." That is to say, shall we seek guidance from the ray of Godhead within our own breast and mind?

Why should I seek a teacher? Why should I want an intermediary to discover God? Is there not all truth within me? Is the desire for a teacher the last desire to be surrendered? Is the running hither and thither in quest of a guide the last step in the wrong direction? Do we not thereby confess that we are seeking within, in our own internal and spiritual being? This is the suspicion that sooner or later will throw a shadow across the road and call us to "Halt." If we fare further, we do but seek outside that guidance—the truth, help, and inspiration—that, in the ultimate, must come from the Divine Self alone. For is not the teacher's work but to lead one to the knowledge of one's own true Self? Such are some of the inwardly prompted questions that naturally arise in an age when the human species is increasingly individualizing its mentality.

Amid this conflict of thoughts, each apparently true, the mind may well reel. But after war comes peace, and the troubled soul can find an honorable solution. It is this: Let us pray daily to the divinity within, and pray as though it were for life itself when in great danger, choosing some words like these: "O, Thou Divinity within this body. Unto thee Love and Obedience. None else does this self know to whom to turn, save Thee. Yet art Thou shrouded in impenetrable darkness. Thou art the object of this search, yet how art Thou to be found? If only through Thy Light in some other human form, some teacher, grant that this being may meet such a one soon, and know him or her as soon as met. But if Thou wish that this self know Thee directly, without another's aid, then must Thou open by Thy grace the gate that leads within, for I am helpless to do so."

A very earnest Western seeker once traveled to an Eastern country in quest of a guru. She selected the monastery of best repute and rented a cottage up on a hill. She sought for tuition from the abbot but her requests were ignored. After six months, as it seemed useless to stay longer, she began arranging to depart and return home. Just then the comprehension struck her, as in a sudden flash, that no one outside herself could do for her the work resulting in self-realization. This seemed to clear her mind and show her a path of self-improvement. She was now ready to depart in peace. But that was the very moment when the abbot unexpectedly came at last to visit her and to tell her she was now ready for his help. So she remained and, thus, began her discipleship. It is significant that the country where this happened was not India.

Real masters ardently wish disciples to attain the state where they can dispense with their services. These masters know that they will help disciples more by giving them the strength to escape from than by leading disciples to depend on them. Every true master delights when disciples begin to walk alone. If they do not have this wish and this delight, then they are not masters but exploiters. It is a fact, which vested interests and selfish exploitation have hidden from many for thousands of years, that divine guidance, inspiration, and help can also come to the aspirant who deliberately walks alone. For our own Overself is the unfailing witness of all our efforts and aspirations and is ever ready to befriend us. The inner light that is always there for us is a safe and reliable light by which we can walk. When we begin to walk by the light of our own unveiled understanding and not by the borrowed lamp of another's, we begin to walk with sure steps. Such a sublime self-reliance is in every way better than the abject dependence on another human being, which passes so often for discipleship.

The few who will gaze on these lines with confidence rather than with contempt, who in default of finding the right teacher and while refusing to accept the wrong one will make the experiment of working with their own natural intelligence, enkindled by their own heartfelt yearning, prayer, and warm devotion toward the Overself, shall find that the divine guidance can unquestionably become a living dynamic within their hearts—wise enough to give them all needful new instruction and strong enough to shape their whole lives. The inward teacher will lead them upward to the realization of their diviner possibilities as well as any outward teacher, or else it will lead them to such a person if available.

After students have taken the decisive step of depending on nobody but their own Overself, they make a strange discovery and one of peculiar importance today when authentic sages are—so far as we know—perhaps a vanished race. The silence begins to speak to them with a new and profounder voice. We refer to the mystical phenomenon known as the "Interior Word." We learn that Truth has never departed from humankind. It is around everyone; it is within us, too. It is our hidden nature. But are we willing to receive it? Are we ready to recognize and to trust it? When we can answer these questions affirmatively, we shall perceive that we need no other teacher than the Overself. Once we awaken to this light, we need henceforth search in no other place than that occupied by our own heart.

Ramakrishna's words, quoted earlier, are supported by a passage in the Arabic writings of Ibn Ul Farid, the thirteenth-century mystical adept of Cairo: "I saw that he who brought me to behold and led me to my spiritual self was I. . . . Even so my prayer was to myself. . . . Here I reached a point from which the intellect recoils before gaining it, where from myself I was being joined and united to myself. . . . And since I was seeking myself from myself, I directed myself to myself, and my soul showed me the way by means of me. Thinkst thou it was another, not thyself, that conversed with thee in the drowsiness of sleep touching various kinds of exalted wisdom?"

FIVE

Ethical Qualifications of the Seeker

WE WHO POSSESS the name and bear the form of humans are to be respected only when reason rises to the ascendant over the animal in our nature. The danger of passions like lust, anger, and animal violence is proverbial, but the blindness of the emotions like attraction and repulsion is often unrecognized. Passion is brought down to defeat by the combined labors of reason and will from our own side and by grace and suffering from beyond ourselves. We have to quell the periodical turbulence of passion until it tires of revolting and gives up the struggle, and we must refuse to be victimized by emotions. The battle against the animal nature is fought inside ourselves. Especially must we learn to fight our emotions. We must give battle at some times to pleasurable feelings, at other times to painful ones. Our lusts and cupidities war against worthier ideals. Continually must we strive to be as truthful in our feelings and as accurate in our emotions as we should already seek to be in our ideas. It is during these periods of emotional strain that we are likely to make faulty decisions and take wrong action.

The exercise of calmness under all circumstances is a definite aid to the student's progress on the path. Out of this unruffled calmness there will come naturally an accurate discernment of values and a balanced judgment.

There are moments of great tribulation or of great temptation when our controls may be shattered. Students must never permit themselves to get so angry about anything that they lose self-control.

Judgments should be dispassionate and disinterested, not conditioned by desires. Appraisals of the most hotly disputed issues will then be balanced and fair, correct, and reasonable. We will not make a negative criticism without at the same time making a positive suggestion.

One of the targets of the philosophic aspirant in the endeavors for self-improvement is liberation from all those emotional prejudices of a personal and communal nature that divide, antagonize, and retard progress. Philosophy makes for a more charitable attitude toward all. Malevolence must yield to goodwill unwarped by prejudices. Such goodwill acts as a solvent of the prejudices, dislikes, frictions, envies, and hatreds that darken social life.

It is not that we should reject emotion from our attitudes (as if we could) but that we should not form attitudes solely in terms of emotion. The emotional appeal is not absent from philosophy, but it is an appeal to our higher and not to our baser emotions. Philosophy does not sterilize emotion but spiritualizes it.

If our thoughts were deprived of all feeling, they would make little positive impression on our minds. Each idea would then carry the same weight, the same importance as another. The thought of a teapot would be in the same category as the thought of truth. So it is not that we are to eliminate feeling from life. It is that we are to control and discipline it, to keep it in its proper place. For a consciousness in which passion or emotion has got the upper hand and from which reason is absent is like an unsubstantial cinema screen world whose objects can be distinguished by sight but not felt by touch. Hence, in this quest for truth, the metaphysical facts must be related together by reason but they must also be made actual by feeling.

As mystics, we must educate our hearts as effectively as we have already educated our intuition. When the workings of emotion get the approval of reason and the sanction of intuition, then are they safe and healthy. Only when passion is bridled and emotion is curbed do we become reconciled with life and discover the meaning of serenity.

The emotion, which in various grades of keenness we call satisfaction, pleasure, joy, felicity, bliss, or happiness, reaches its fullest volume and loftiest quality when it deserts the lower self altogether and expresses only the higher one. Our thoughts about these higher things must be blended with feelings about them. But the feelings must be in consonance with the ideas. These noble moods are not to be put in the same category as the sloppy emotionalistic ones that merely disfigure rather than express the mystical life.

Seekers must learn the art of being their own masters under every kind of circumstance. The way of self-overcoming is an upward one, a difficult one, but it is as essential to the quest as the smoother way of giving ourselves up to emotional ecstasies in meditation. What must be done is to assert dominion over the thoughts that would drag us down, the feelings that would tear us, and the many foolish selves that would misrepresent us. It is not enough to try to deal with the manifestations of the lower self by creative thought alone. It is also necessary to make a parallel effort of the will, a self-denying endeavor to lift action onto a higher level, an active tearing struggle to resist what seems to be a veritable part of our own being. Not only must we control the actions that seek to satisfy desires against our better judgment, but even the day-dreaming that seeks the same objective.

We should beware of the first onset of merely negative and viciously destructive or shamefully egoistic emotions. It is easier to stop the life of tender shoots than of maturer ones. This is especially true of emotions like jealousy, pique, wounded pride, bitter resentment, and hot anger.

We must discipline ourselves to face the vagaries of fortune and surmount the vicissitudes of life. Such a self-discipline will provide our youthful years with more security, our aged ones with more dignity. Those who do not arrive at this self-discipline from within, peaceably and voluntarily, will have it imposed from without, compulsorily and violently.

Prolonged association with certain people may deeply alter our character and powerfully divert us from our general direction. It depends upon us either to accept or to resist their influence. We must be on our guard against the misdirection of our forces and the deflection of our aspirations. They can be correctly led only if we follow the counsels of philosophy. Just as the best when corrupted becomes the worst, so strength when misdirected becomes weakness. We must seek and find the proper balancing and safeguarding factors.

To the habit of orderly thinking, which education may have given us, we must add the habit of disinterested thinking, which in its perfect form philosophy alone can give.

We will neither take refuge in complacent escapism nor give ourselves up to helpless despair. We will look the situation in the face, calmly and steadily. We will approach people and events, ideas, and problems, not as one belonging to any of the conventional orthodoxies but as a detached truth-seeker. We must see things in their true light without the deceptions or distortions provided by greed, hatred, lust, prejudice, and the like. Personal reactions to world events must be brought into line with the rest of our truth-seeking endeavor.

Those who can use their thinking power in the purest way—

that is to say, unbiased, undeflected, unweighted, unegoistic—are extremely rare. Yet the philosophic training seeks to lead us to do just this.

It should be our aim to retain and sustain our ideals whatever the surroundings in which we happen to find ourselves. In a society animated by narrow prejudices and unworthy selfishnesses, we must steadfastly keep our moral integrity. We must strive to maintain a strict integrity of character henceforth, as being a vital part of the path toward the Overself. Thus the quest is not easy and not always pleasant. We must defend the integrity of our mental life against all physical foes, human or environmental.

We do not progress by yielding to weakness that masquerades as virtue, but by nurturing strength even though it bears a disagreeable face.

It is not enough only to discover the principles that secretly control human life. It is also necessary for the student not to contravene the precepts that arise from them, nor to act at variance with them in daily conduct. These principles are not to be obstinately supported at one time only to be suddenly sacrificed at another.

As our character matures and intuition develops, the soundness of the ideals for which we work becomes plainer than ever. When we are really in earnest about this quest, there will come a time when we will have to make a heroic stand for its moral principles, when we must refuse to sacrifice them for the sake of a shifting passing advantage. We will reach a stage where we will not only refuse to violate this code of ethics but will refuse even though we could gain greatly thereby, or even though our violation could never be discovered by others.

Aspirants should know that if they have been true to the injunctions of the teaching, they will sooner or later receive deliverance from difficulties. Our steps may still be halting, our minds still unsure of themselves, yet with the passage of time we will find that definite progress has been made.

We will reach a bodily age and mental ripeness when certain truths will be clearer to our view and less repulsive to our feelings. Of these we should consider three: the illusory value of sex; the need to subordinate emotion to reason; and the reality of the invisible, intangible Overself. We should meditate again and again upon these things if we want inner peace.

Our success in life can no longer be measured adequately by externals alone but must be measured also by how far we have succeeded in purifying the heart, developing intelligence, unfolding intuition, and attaining balance.

SIX

Cleansing of the Emotions

IT IS NOT ENOUGH for students to utter the petition or make the demand that their Soul shall reveal itself. This is necessary—and moreover in a sustained form—but we have also to provide the requisite conditions for such a revelation. Having accepted the philosophic way of Soul-realization as the higher purpose of earthly life, we should next consider what we must do to fulfill it. That will depend on both our inward state and outward circumstances. If we have mastered the few basic principles and accepted the chief ethical ideals, we must learn to apply philosophy to our own particular personal requirements. Something more than a mere intellectual interest in its teachings is needed if we wish to honor them. We ought not to expect to receive enlightenment from the Higher Self, much less be possessed by it, before we have established within ourselves the proper conditions for such a divine visitation.

Such a condition will not arise of itself. To prepare it, we must impose some moral and mystical discipline. The initial weak desire for self-betterment and character-building must grow into a strong, mastering passion. Aspirants must exceed their own best, go beyond their own past. We may not loll in indolent complacency but should begin to strengthen our moral impulses, to build up character, and to train thinking. Leaving behind all dilettantism, we must strive vigorously and persistently toward clearer self-understanding and emotional detachment. A strict endeavor after self-improvement, a continuous effort after self-purification, must also be made. It is most necessary for the philosophic aspirant to aim at such moral self-improvement, to develop the exercise of character, and to cultivate the chief virtues preached by the great prophets of all religions. A well-balanced equipment is as valuable on this quest as is a well-balanced effort, which is neither too feeble nor too violent. The higher will is latent within us and is developed only by recognition, submission, and exercise. We ought to feel ashamed if a single day has passed without its proper share of mystical meditation, devotional prayer, and moral endeavor, disciplining the mind and cleansing the heart.

Our first duty is to get rid of the last traces of animality. Hence mystical tradition has called this early phase of a spiritual career the phase of purification. Yes! The Higher Self will eventually come and enter our consciousness if only we will prepare the requisite conditions of a still mind and a pure heart. But this we will not be able to do successfully unless we love It more than we love the world. For the first condition calls upon us to surrender our thoughts in meditation and the second, our desires in renunciation.

There are two factors that are noticeably absent from modern life and that must be brought into it if it is to become spiritually worthwhile. They are contemplation and renunciation. While the senses completely rule the mind, ignorance is its necessary companion. While the heart is totally given up to outward things, suffering is its intermittent visitor. Only by disciplining the one and introverting the other can the light of understanding dawn and the calm of balance prevail.

Yet it is needful here to beware of extreme views. There are fanatics for virtue who say that no one should sit down to meditate until their character has been thoroughly purified. There are fanatics for meditation who assert that virtue is itself only an effect, of which meditation is the cause. Philosophy is more reasonable because it is more balanced. It requires the side-by-side parallel endeavor of both these ways. It says, practice meditation but purify and ennoble character still more at the same time. For the aspirant's work begins and ends with moral re-education even more than with mysticism. We must eliminate weaknesses and acquire virtues.

For most beginners it is often more important to better the character than to practice meditation. This is because, firstly, the results of meditation may be good or bad according as the character is good or bad. Secondly, the success obtained with meditation will be less or more, according to the presence or absence of virtues or weaknesses. Thirdly, that which stands in the way of union with the Overself is the ego-self, which has to be weakened and thinned, little by little, through the purification of character, until the great final battle with it can take place in the inner mystically developed stillness.

This ego-self is made up of two parts. The first includes the emotional desires and mental attachments for things or people in the outside world. The second includes those elements that we share through the body with the animals. Thus the first part is human and the second is animal. The two together constitute the lower egoistic self.

Our first disciplinary act cannot escape being a painful one. It is to take out of the heart all those instincts and passions that bind us to the animal self. We may mitigate the pain by extending the time of the operation. If we are young in years, probably we will. But if we are middle-aged, still more if old, we cannot afford to delay. In particular, all the malevolent emotions and aggressive attitudes have to be thoroughly cleared out from our natures; we will have to perform some drastic surgery upon them.

But that is only the beginning of the work. The aim at the next stage is to discover and rid ourselves of the evil qualities and secret attachments that bar the way to our Soul. There are several great tempters that must be overcome if we are to achieve inward freedom. Among them are the ambition to gain power, the desire to increase possessions, the craving to become famous, and the lust to gratify sex. "Give up desires," is the essence of the discipline enjoined by the Bhagavad Gita, the New Testament, and the Buddhist Tripitaka scriptures. Why? There are two reasons. First, the mind must be made free to seek the Truth. Second, the will must be set free to express it. People who are controlled by any desire and who cannot control it have a warped outlook. They unconsciously demand that Truth should conform with their desires. They cannot "see straight," cannot apply themselves wholeheartedly to inquiring into Truth. Philosophic discipline is the best method of freeing a human being from such distortions in mind and feeling and rendering us truly fit to ascertain Truth. It detaches us from worldly ties, gives us an independent outlook and trains us to view things without personal passion or suggested bias.

A hard precept is the instruction to "kill out desire" found in *Light on the Path*.* There is no harm in recognizing our needs and calculating how to provide for them. What we have to do is to distinguish between the lower and the higher desires, between ignoble and noble ones, between those that harm our fellow creatures and those that help them. We must oppose the one, accept the other. There

---

Light on the Path is a standard of Theosophical literature written by Mabel Collins in 1885.

are various ways that, combined, will help us rule our lower desires and bring them to the service of this quest of the Overself. On the physical side, we should foster willpower, practice self-denial, discipline our bodies by occasional short fasts, cease from frivolities that stimulate desires and nourish passion. On the intellectual side, we should study the metaphysics and ethics of philosophy and lift ourselves regularly above the very realm in which desires operate.

There is inspiration and power—not merely information and argument—in the study of true metaphysics. These intellectual endeavors, this reading and study, these reflections and musings, are necessary and useful and will in time begin to have their effect not only upon our knowledge but also upon our character. Not only are they uplifting, but they are also purifying. Not only do they explain the presence of lower desires and animal passions in us, but they also contribute toward checking them. Not only do they give the reasons why we should make our characters better, but they constantly give powerful suggestions to realize this betterment. Thus, if our doubts and misconceptions will be slowly cleared, our morals and motives will be slowly bettered.

Another well-known precept of the ethics of mysticism, which is dangerously open to misunderstanding or easily liable to non-acceptance, is the Bhagavad Gita's injunction not to look for the results and fruits of our actions. The correct meaning is that we are not to be personally so attached to the results that our mind's peace and our heart's happiness utterly depend on them. We must appraise our needs correctly and use our forces worthily. The Gita teaching does not absolve us from this duty. This will certainly lead to results, and we shall certainly be responsible for them. The teaching does not mean that we are to stand aside and do nothing and so avoid personal entanglements; indeed, the whole keynote of the book opposes such a futile conception, such glorifying of complete inertia. It means that we are to stand aside from attachments and clingings.

The practical side of this quest begins by a slow turning away from the old unconsidered life, a deliberate rearranging of unsatisfactory habits, a voluntary cutting-out of desires that weaken or degrade the character, and a constant analytic self-examination to detect faults in thought, feeling, and conduct. This effort has not only to be started in real earnest but also carried to a certain point before authentic spiritual, as distinct from psychical, experience may be expected. Any system of ethics that is based on spiritual fact must always discipline, and sometimes oppose, our natural desires. For a time the animal in us must be crucified, the human mortified.

The full if distant goal is to liberate ourselves from entire submission to the calls of the flesh and the turmoils of the mind, from animalistic urges and humanistic graspings. We have to pass from the common state of willingness to accept the flesh as our master to the uncommon state of rebellion against it. The process of self-cleansing necessarily involves the acceptance of discipline, the practice of penance or asceticism, and even the showing of moral courage. We have to deny this or that thing to the body for a time, in some cases even for all time. We have to curb the vehemence of deep-rooted long-lived feelings. We have to set about the reversal of ancient mental habits and abandon emotions that are instinctive in human nature. It would be almost impossible to continue in these endeavors were it not for the stimulus we receive from glimpses of the ideal, the longing we feel to transform it into a reality, and the reality of grace.

For these controls, the exercise of modified asceticism—the practice of a certain austerity—is indispensable. It must be sincere and sane, however, which means it must be first, imposed from within by intuitive promptings and second, temporary and limited. We must determine of what kind it shall be and how much. We must impose it and not anyone else. For the discipline must be demanded from within by our own Soul, which best knows what we need at the time. Sacrifice in some form is demanded, but it is not demanded before we are ready for it. Animal instinct and human greed will have to submit themselves to spiritual intuition, but they need not submit prematurely. Thus philosophy pursues neither an impossible perfection on the one hand nor an impracticable asceticism on the other.

Desire is necessary to human life and the spiritual desires do not extinguish desire, but only give it another and higher direction. If there were no desire there could be no universe, for God could not make this universe without the desire to do so.

Everything that hinders the divine will's passage through our hearts and lives must eventually be cast out. What these hindrances are will be made known from time to time by both inward promptings and external events. We have to affiliate our lower will with our higher one; the two must be brought to work in unison. All our thoughts and feelings are to be permeated with this diviner motive. A steady self-discipline, a constant obedience to ideals, a faithful carrying-out of spiritual duties—these are demands upon the will. To meet them we will have to harden and strengthen it. The task of making ourselves strong enough to ride turbulent passions and restless thoughts is not a weakling's one. When passions and desires and instincts conflict with our ideals, there is no way out except to fight and overcome them. We cannot afford to leave our inner lives at their mercy.

The purification of the sense-life, the training of the thought-life, and the bridling of the emotional-life constitute the great preliminary cycle of the quest. Consequently, it involves and cannot escape being a cycle of irritation, tension, conflict, and suffering. It is true to say that the consciousness of people engaged in this quest swings like the pendulum of a clock, to and fro, in the struggle between earthly passion and spiritual aspiration, between egoistic pettiness and ethical grandeur, and between contrary moods. This cannot be helped. We have become a field of struggle for powerful antagonists, with nothing less than our Soul for the prize. The animal and the angel are both in ourselves. We discover that the lower emotions are more easily aroused than stilled; subduing them will be accomplished only at the end of a long period of time. Most people find it too much trouble to engage in self-improvement or too fatiguing to do more than talk about it. They are hardly to be blamed. This arduous enterprise, once started, never really comes to an end. How long it will last cannot be predicted in a general statement, for it will differ with different individuals. Sometimes it is a matter of a couple of years, more often of several, not seldom of a whole lifetime. The achievement of a reasonably desireless state is necessarily the travail of many lives on earth.

The process of detaching from the lower nature is also comparable to the process of extracting teeth. But there is no spiritual anesthetic here to mitigate its painfulness. Nevertheless it may help to endure the pain to remember: first, that quite a number of Easterners and Westerners have demonstrated that it is possible to spiritualize mental energies, reorient disturbing passions, and elevate strong emotions; and second, that if the search for our Soul begins in agony, the finding ends in joy. The emotional chill that the teaching of renunciation always gives the trembling beginner will one day be succeeded by the emotional freedom that the same teaching gives the more mature disciple. It is misery for the ego to renounce its desires. The feeling of unbearable sacrifice weighs heavily upon it. Yet it is happiness for that same ego when, at long last and by the Overself's grace, desires renounce it, for the feeling of liberation from their burden will uplift it.

To enable us to free ourselves from these lower emotional hindrances and attain this objective of ruling animal appetites, a systematic training must be employed, a course of discipline must be passed through. The power of unruled desire in us is strong and terrible but it can be negated by a twofold process: observing and analyzing constantly those harmful deeper consequences that most people ignore, and dwelling constantly on the benefits and attractions of the opposite state. We will need to use the service of both analytic reflection and creative imagination in our meditation exercises; of contrite penitence, humble prayer, and lofty aspiration in our devotional ones; of short occasional fasts and a meatless diet in our physical regime.

It is not easy for anyone to disentangle from animal tendencies. But anyone may discipline the will by degrees—out of weakness into strength and out of animal subjugation into holy governance. Therefore ascetic disciplines, practiced for short limited periods and repeated at convenient intervals, are prescribed by philosophy to assist and quicken the process. But they are never prescribed alone. Suitable meditations are coupled with them, for the real battle occurs within the mind. Through constant thought and repeated aspiration, we must make ourselves so familiar with the higher ideals that obedience to them becomes second nature. We have to learn by severe discipline how to follow higher intuitions rather than lower instincts, how to greet the tempting images that enter our minds, how to dissect them at once and separate the warm emotional temptations from the cold thought-out facts. If our animal tendencies and egoistic fixations prevent a full surrender to the Higher Self and even disturb our faith in the possibility of ever achieving such a surrender, this is still no reason to fall into despondency. By prayer we may invoke grace. By grace we may conquer self.

It is plainly not the ego's own will that is either willing to turn upon, or be capable of subjugating, itself. From what source then is the power drawn to execute the Overself's commands? There is indeed a higher will that transcends the ordinary one. It is a necessary though painful experience of this quest to arrive at the humiliating discovery that, do what we will, the ultimate conquest of the animal part of our nature is beyond our control. We may have periods when it would seem that this conquest has been effected, but an unexpected happening or a sudden incursion of thoughts will disillusion us. This self-discovery will be most valuable in the end, however, if it leads us to avow our inability and to acknowledge our imperfections, if it makes our ego utterly humble. For then, in our anguish, we will have to seek help from a higher power, be it the Overself or someone who has learned to live in the Overself.

We will, in short, have to seek and pray for grace. And this, when it comes, will be truly amazing. For we will feel ourselves being lifted above animal instincts and physical passions to a higher level of our being. And it will be accomplished without any struggle on our part—indeed, with wonderful ease. We no longer weakly accept the negative suggestions of undeveloped people and evil spirits, of our own past tendencies or low environment, but the higher will, of its own accord, rises up inside us and rebuts or rejects them. We who could not extirpate the passions by our own efforts will find them extirpated for us by the Overself. The attainment of this sublimer consciousness automatically delivers us from their chains.

We will know when we are progressing by the sharpened recognition of our own yieldings to the lower self and by the deepened insight into their characteristic degrees, operations, and origins. Thus on this philosophic path the seeker is not called on formally and peremptorily to renounce any desire; for, little by little, the desires will themselves renounce us! The power of the evil principle over us becomes weaker and weaker, the power of the Divine Self stronger and stronger. As this Self takes more and more possession of our characters, passions become subdued, earthly desires become less and less troublesome. When we feel ourselves sufficiently advanced to make the test, we may even deliberately imagine alluring situations and attractive forms and note how we react to them. But to attempt this at too early a stage would be an error. We may mentally work out a temptation in advance and pursue it to its inevitable consequences. Thus by purely rational and imaginative processes, we may obtain the benefit of such an experience without receiving the troubles and sufferings that, in many cases, develop from it.

THE TRUE MEANING OF DESIRELESSNESS

We feel our insufficiency and incompleteness. All our ventures in friendship and love, marriage and association, are really strivings to remove this feeling. We never succeed fully or for long, however. This is so and must be so, because what we are and what we are seeking outside of ourselves exists only inside ourselves. The missing factor is none other than our own living Soul.

Humans are chained to earth by a score of desires. When we engage in the quest, we see then that all these sweet desires end in sorry captivities, and if we are to escape from the misery of a divided self, we must disengage from them. Hence the strength of all our desire-being is to be withdrawn from its former objects and reoriented inward to the Divine Soul. Even the body is to become a mere instrument for our wisest thought and best will, not for our lowest nature. This is the great contest to which we are called.

If we have to worry constantly about the sustenance and shelter of the body, we become preoccupied with it just as much as if we have too much, too many possessions, and become preoccupied with them. So the ideal is to find the middle ground between too much and too little in order to liberate the mind from continual concern with the body and its possessions.

Let both the physical body and the things it owns be given their rightful place—no more, no less—so that they may be made to subserve the higher purpose of life, which is to fulfill the quest of the Overself.

Yet we live in a highly acquisitive world. That is why there have been and still are so many nominal but so few real Buddhists and Christians. For both Buddha and Jesus insisted that the way to the goal to which they called humanity lay through giving up the hungers for possessions, position, sex, and self-assertion. There is no durable happiness in these things but only the illusion of it. Nobody can put a term to the acquisition of better status, more wealth, increased fame, greater glory, extra possessions. It is a game easier to start than to stop. Because desires grow as they are fed, we will never have enough. Today a thing is a luxury; tomorrow it becomes a necessity. Today that is superfluous; tomorrow it is indispensable. We must ration our desires if we want inner peace. The more we increase them, the more we have to struggle to satisfy them. Until we get this clear in our minds, we shall not get peace in our hearts. There is spiritual realization only for those in whom the grasping hands of the ego are forever withdrawn and the fires of passion have subsided into the ashes of renunciation. What we count our best possessions are in the highest region of our minds and the deepest region of our hearts.

These truths hit hardest, perhaps, in the personal love that we seek to give to or get from others. For we will have to acquire the power to trample resolutely on our own emotions, if and whenever the Overself calls upon us to do so. Indeed, the entire course of the preliminary ascetic discipline is one long sacrifice. Coolly to stand aside from emotions like personal love and sexual affection, ruthlessly to dissect their nature and unyieldingly to repel their invasion is the hardest of all its ordeals. The application of mentalism to such dissection may help a little. All desire is really mental. Were it not for the images that it forms in the mind, no desired object would attract us. When a young man falls deeply in love with a particular young woman, he is really deeply in love with his idea of her. In the moment that he yields the mind's calm to any disturbing passion, be it jealousy, sex, or anger, he yields it to an idea. He must learn to control his ideas if he is to control his conduct. And by learning to check imagination, he learns to control desire.

"All dependence on another is misery, dependence on oneself is happiness," declared the Indian lawgiver Manu several thousand years ago. To the extent that we depend on others for happiness, to that extent we are likely to lose it one day through death, desertion, or disease. And because normal sexual passion is entirely dependent, it is also entirely deceptive. If we seek a happiness that will stay with us under all circumstances, then we must not seek it from another man or woman, else we invite disappointment. We must seek it at its enduring source—the Overself. We who depend on others for happiness will never enjoy its enduring reality but only its ephemeral appearance. Human love may be withdrawn from us after a time but the divine love never. We must learn how to live without feeling the absolute need of someone else. Where there is such dependence, there can be no durable happiness. The moment we make another person the chief basis for happiness, we have opened a door to possible unhappiness. We should look for supreme happiness to no embodied creature. For such a happiness, in its truest sense, cannot be found unless it be found in and from oneself. This is because it is to be got only from the Divine, which is pure Spirit, and because it is attainable only through the gateway of one's own heart, not through another's. The quest of ideal love, let alone perfect companionship, can never be satisfied by any woman or man but only by the Soul hidden within. The Soul indeed is the true Beloved who, ever patient and ever faithful, waits for the time when we shall discover and woo it. The love that we can find in the Soul will not depend on a changeable human mood for its existence, will not be affected by the conditions or accident of human flesh, but will be perfectly trustworthy and serenely sure. More, it will always be there, always be more faithful than any human love could ever be. If we pass from this world into another, or even fifty other worlds, still it will remain our loyal companion. It must be. For it comes not from a different, a separate entity; it comes from our own inmost Self and is an eternal attribute of our eternal Soul. The truth brings with it great serenity and also great independence. We are no longer at the mercy of others for our happiness.

The growing disciple will learn to live a strange paradoxical existence. Events will so occur, the course of our external life will so flow, men and women will so behave toward us that in the end we will be driven away from externals and forced to find reality, truth, love, friendships, possessions, beauty, satisfactions, and even spiritual guidance within—in the worlds of imagination, of thought, and of that which transcends both. In the end we will have to accept the fact that human solitude is inescapable, that the human Soul is inviolable, that the separation between one human being and another cannot be overcome in reality but only in appearance.

We who have found the Beloved within are not afraid to be alone. We are always gratefully ready to accept the company and friendship, the affection and devotion that others may wish to give us, but we can live without them if fate bids it be so. That person has attained to practical wisdom who has attained to inward self-sufficiency, who does his or her best for all yet expects nothing from any of them, whose work contributes its utmost to life but whose heart expects little from it. Because such a one expects little from others, whatever does come will be thankfully accepted as a bonus but not as anything more. One looks only to oneself for happiness and relies only on oneself for achievement. "What one gets without any expectation is like nectar," wrote Swami Sahajananda, a Kathiawar master, in a letter to his disciples more than a century ago.

The Divine Self asks for nothing less than the whole of our hearts for a sacrifice utter and complete. In return it will give us the consciousness of its presence, the awareness of its love, and the blessedness of its time-free state. If we are to attain and feel intensely its heavenly peace, we can do so only by buying it with a heavenly desirelessness. Nature gives everything at a price. Much that we believe to be a part of ourselves must go. This process of divesting ourselves of the lower desires and emotions is agonizing yet indispensable. We must come to the point of desiring to be possessed by the Divine Soul above all other desires.

Such a hard counsel is not for the many who feel no hunger for truth, no readiness for a higher life. The enslavement by body, senses, passions, and thoughts is supposed by them to be the natural state of humankind—so weak have they become. Yet only those who have gained self-freedom and self-mastery are really natural and perfectly at ease. Most people are so strong in earthly habits and so weak in spiritual longing that the disciplinary requirements of the quest seem too forbidding and too unrealizable. To such people, the quest's ideal seems as cold and as implacable as the snowy heights of the Himalayas. No! This counsel is tendered to disciples only, that is, to those who have voluntarily put themselves under a discipline for the sake of finding the Soul. It is tendered to the person who has made the great decisions; who negatively has renounced animal appetite and put aside human desires; who positively has accepted the Intangible Reality as the chief Good in this life and the Overself as the true ego of one's being. An ethos of desirelessness first baffles and then repels the modern mind. Its disparagement of wants that are natural, ambitions that are legitimate, and possessions that are civilizing does not seem to deserve discussion because it does not seem to make sense. There is a short step only from the intellectual position that such an ethos is insane to the emotional position that it is inhuman.

What is the practical value of such an ethos? How far is it requisite to the needs of modern people? These questions can be properly answered only if we look to our terms. First, we should not confuse necessities with wants. We should come to a clearer understanding of what is and is not essential to life, so that we can simplify and elevate it. Second, let it be specially noted that the call is to a renunciation that is essentially of an inward character. We may keep possessions outwardly if we forsake them inwardly. If called upon to abandon everything, it is only sometimes that this is to be done externally, although always to be done internally.

The declaration that entry into the kingdom of heaven can be effected only by those unweighted with possessions is a true one. But the possessions referred to are not external ones; they are wholly interior, intangible, and invisible. Such a person is secretly dead to the world even while apparently moving, working, enjoying, and suffering in the midst of it. Such is the true desireless state. We have to learn the paradoxical art of having natural desires like others and yet being as if we did not really have them. That is to say, we may possess them insofar as we are human beings with human needs—although with us they will be simplified, disciplined, and elevated—but at heart's core we are ready at every moment to desert them instantly. Thus we establish a sane equilibrium between the wish to possess and the will to renounce.

The most satisfactory attitude to adopt is the one that the Buddha had to adopt after experiencing both extremes of the princely life in a palace and the Spartan life of an ascetic. In the end he taught that the middle way was best, making use of things without becoming entangled in them. "When thou hast surrendered all this, then thou mayst enjoy," says the Isha Upanishad. Renunciation need not prevent us from loving friends, need not deter us from valuing comforts, need not deny us the use of clever inventions, luxurious homes, and artistic creations. But it will permit all this only when and to the extent that it does not trespass upon our time with the Divine, our devotion to it, and our choice of it.

Philosophic discipline is not ascetic discipline: It does not ask us to renounce all ties of friendship, family, and marriage, all affection for other human beings. We may keep the ties and the affections. It asks only that we shall free them from possessiveness, that we shall care deeply for others along with, and not in denial of, the Divine, that we shall maintain all lesser loves inside its larger love and not be imprisoned inside them. We are not required to abandon worldly life but to spiritualize it, not called upon to renounce personal relationships but to approach them from a new point of view. It would be a sad error to think that this passage from attachments to detachment, from earthly entanglements to heavenly ones, is made by destroying human relationships and chilling human affections. The actuality is that we become more loving in our behavior to family or friends and not less. But it is a love of higher quality than before, purer, less selfish, and more benign.

Purity of heart means in philosophy the forsaking of all possessions and all persons, not before the world's gaze but before God's. There is peace for those who have entered the desireless state. So long as they are inwardly dead to the world, they may outwardly remain active in it. Neither an external asceticism nor an external abandonment of worldly life is what matters or is called for so much as an internal detachment. When ascetic renunciation has fulfilled its inner purpose, when it has helped to bring the animal self to subjugation and the personal self to submission, it may itself be renounced if we choose to do so. For it is not an end, only a means to an end. Once our thoughts and feelings are sufficiently pure, the value of external sacrificial discipline drops to little. The needs of the human body and the human entity tenanting it may be satisfied on two conditions: first, that they are disciplined by reason; second, that they are not allowed to obscure the needs of human life's spiritual and ultimate goal. These conditions we have fulfilled.

When we have truly entered into the desireless state, when we no longer feel the need for anyone or anything, when the feeling that wells up continuously from our inmost heart is self-completion and self-contentment, we will perceive how pitiable is the tragic state of those who, still earthbound, walk with fettered hands and clanking feet, but know it not and even glory in their bondage. The twelve labors of Hercules are an allegorical description of the aspirant's struggle with the lower nature and adverse forces.

Beyond the clinging to possessions and the yielding to passions, the quester must travel still further. Even the overcoming of our ego's desires in these directions will not bring us to the goal, though it will advance us far beyond the captive multitudes.

We still need to penetrate to the depths of contemplation, where all is emptiness profound, where personal identity is dissolved, and where God alone is.

We then need to learn the art of bringing all this into relation with our common everyday existence, with our activities in the world. We further need to make a fresh orientation toward the intellect, replacing our contempt for and detachment from it by a constructive, positive, and integrative attitude.

When this period of self-training is at an end, we will possess the capacity to attend adequately to whatever duty, work, matter, or pleasure our faculties are called upon to attend to, and yet the moment it is finished, to dismiss it so utterly from our mind that it is as if it had never been. With that we will return to unflagging spontaneous concentration upon, and abidance in, the inner Self.

A LIFE OF SERENITY AND WONDER

When so far as is humanly possible we have achieved this independence of externals, when we live from and are true to our own inmost being, we discover a plausible and perennial satisfaction the earthly person never knows.

Whoever fights and succeeds in overcoming the lower nature becomes filled with the serenity and wonder of the higher. The period of tormenting stress and internal division will come to a sudden end, to be followed by a period of satisfying calm and internal unity. The intermittent or personal conflict that goes on in so many hearts will be abolished in our own. We would be foolish indeed to sacrifice for a lower satisfaction the insight, calm, and power we have gained at such great cost and after so many hard conflicts. The sacrifices that in our novitiate seemed so enormous to make are now, in our proficiency, quite effortless to accomplish.

When the struggle with passions and thoughts is brought to a triumphant end, a great tranquillity settles in the heart. The animalistic life has gone out of us. The angelic life has entered. The intellectualist tumult has been silenced. The impulses no longer war within. Indescribable is the serenity of being so self-contained. When the individual consciousness is thus separate from the passions, desires, emotions, and ideas that agitate it, serenity comes to pervade it. And then we will discover the great paradox, that for those who can inwardly, willingly, and secretly renounce the world before the grave forces us to renounce it outwardly, unwillingly, and openly, the world is truly ours and will lie at our feet. This has been pithily stated by Patanjali in his *Yoga Aphorisms,* the first recorded textbook on yoga:

Or the mind-stuff reaches the stable state by having as its object a mind-stuff freed from passion. (1.37)

His mastery extends from the smallest atom to the greatest magnitude. (1.40)

We may match these words with the mystical statement of Jesus: "He who loseth his life shall gain it." In a different way, this yet has somewhat the same meaning as Patanjali's remarks. For in the mystic's highest experience, that of the nihilistic Void, he or she is divested of the entire personal ego, of every thought, thing, and desire. Mystics possess nothing and are nothing. Nevertheless they have put themselves in a position where, because the Void is the source of everything, everything may be granted. Thus paradoxically, by giving up all, they gain all.

Swami Vivekananda* has said:

When the world is given up, what remains? What is meant? You can have your wife; you certainly do not have to abandon her; but you are to see God in your wife. Give up your children—what does that mean? To turn them out of doors? Certainly not. But see God in your children . . . This is what Vedanta teaches: Give up the world which you have conjectured, a false world of our own creation. Open your eyes, it was a dream, a *maya*. What existed was the Lord himself.

What is meant by giving up desires? How will life go on? The solution is this: not that you should not have property, not that you should not have things which are necessary and even things which are luxuries—have all that you want; only know the truth

*Swami Vivekananda (1863–1902) was the chief disciple of the famous nineteenth-century Indian sage Ramakrishna and a leader in introducing Vedanta and Yoga to the Western world.

about property: that it does not belong to anybody. Have no idea of proprietorship, possession. All belong to the Lord.

If we understand the giving up of the world in its old crude sense then it would come to this: that we must not work—that we must be idle, sitting like lumps of earth, neither thinking nor doing anything. But that is not what is meant. We must work. So do your work, says Vedanta, putting God into everything and knowing It to be in everything. When desires are thus purified, through God, they bring no evil, they bring no misery.

In the foregoing pages the subject has been considered from the standpoint of students and aspirants. Let them note that the ethical problems and mental conflicts that it touches do not arise for the sage. For at the very moment when the student attains supreme enlightenment, whatever desires and passions may be left fall away of their own accord. Whatever he or she does in external conduct thenceforth cannot alter this inward state of sublime if secret detachment in which a sage perpetually rests. Sages may play total ascetics if they choose or may play complete worldlings, but their own exalted status remains unaffected by either role. In renouncing the ego, they have renounced everything. They have reached a point where there is nothing else left to renounce. The desire to achieve desirelessness has been fulfilled. A wonderful feeling of liberation floods their hearts, a vast serenity stills their minds. An intense and enduring satisfaction with the Overself is present. Nothing else in the world seems so worth having, for having this they feel they have what is most worthwhile in life.

SEVEN

Surrender of the Ego

PHILOSOPHY IS UNINTERESTED in flattering people or in pandering to vanity. Therefore it begins the practical side of its discipline by pointing out defects, faults, and shortcomings, and by opening our eyes at last to our weaknesses, incapacities, and complexes that hitherto have been unconscious or disguised. To go forward safely on the path, we need to be cured of fanatical obsessions and irrationalities. We may think that eradication of personal faults has little to do with finding the true Self, but this is not correct. These very faults arise out of the false conception of the "I." Moreover the eradication is suggested not only to help overcome such false conceptions but also to help us become better servants of humanity.

It is true that we cannot help being what we are, that outward circumstances and inward nature, karmic tendencies, and past experiences have combined to shape our character. But only if we are honest with ourselves, if we cease hiding ugly faults and start bringing them into the full light, have we a chance to make solid progress on the quest. We will do well to know what the ego is really like before we attempt to know what the Overself is like. The ruthless searching into our complexes and trends, hidden vanities and desires, is a valuable preparation. We should probe for those of which we have been hitherto quite unaware.

While this constant scrutiny of motives, this searching analysis of character is shirked or feared, egotism is able to disguise itself, subtly turning the most altruistic situations to its own advantage and unsuspectedly satisfying its desires even when seeming not to do so. When allowed to intrude into our observations of life, it makes us fallible, doubtful, distorted, or wrong. The ego must be flattened and even, if necessary, punctured!

That which matters is inspiration and motive. Is the deed prompted by the ego? Or is it prompted by the Overself? Does it seek personal gain? Or does it seek to render altruistic service? The pattern of duty may sometimes be unclear, but the prompting of egotism may always be unmasked. It is easier to overcome the bias of temperament, which, after all, is only a surface thing, than the bias of egotism, which, too often, is so deeply concealed as to be quite invisible. These unconscious purposes operate quite effectively in their own way, and much of the conscious activity shows their influence to the trained observer.

Students must begin with the lowest opinion of themselves if they are to end one day with the highest. On no account should we fall into the common blunder of deeming ourselves more advanced than we really are, for this will lead to failure. Let us not too soon regard ourselves as among the privileged elect, lest we become spiritually proud or morally conceited. In this matter we should heed the counsel of an old Hindustani Indian proverb: "Extend your feet according to the length of your sheet." To wear such rose-colored glasses as will magnify the good into the best serves no other purpose than self-deception. Lapses from the path as well as achievements on it should be reviewed; the self-humiliation thus caused must be accepted and not avoided by a retreat into cynicism or by side-stepping into hypocrisy. The student must have the humility to acknowledge these faults and the willingness to drive them out.

If, for instance, we will only have the moral strength, the little-prized power of renunciation, to desert the lower ego in all its unfriendly differences, disputes, irritations, and troubled relationships with others, we will be compensated by spiritual satisfaction, by a quickened growth of inward being that will far outweigh the initial cost to personal feeling. When we learn, painfully, slowly, and falteringly, to put the lower ego aside in all considerations, reflections, and decisions, we learn one of the greatest lessons that life has to teach. And if we have the strength to oppose our own egos and the greatness to deny our own ambitions, we have crossed the threshold of renunciation.

Unillumined people have no greater enemy than their own lower egos, as illumined people have no greater friend than their own higher selves. Not only is the lower nature our greatest enemy, it is also our subtlest one. It will pretend and deceive, mask and disguise, twist and turn in so cunning a way that quite often we will not know it from our greatest friend, which is also within us.

Aspirants must take the greatest care about their motives and watch them well. The ego is the real enemy on the path, the mountain that cannot be moved by faith but only by agonizing surrender. But the agony is diminished when, through appropriate instruction, we come to understand how illusory the "I" really is. Without vigilance it is easy to go astray in such matters. The dividing line is often fine. We must be aware of the undeniable dangers, the tremendous temptations, and the pitfalls around us. How hard it seems for us to give ourselves to our own guardian angels, how easy to give ourselves to our besetting demons.

Students must beware of the cunning disguises of the retreating ego. We must beware of its self-flattery pretending to be the Overself's flattery. We must beware of any "mission" to which we are appointed. If the inner voice promises us a remarkable future, whether a spiritual attainment or a worldly triumph, disbelieve it. Only if it makes us humbler and meeker should we believe it.

The ego will resist repeatedly in a long-drawn struggle. It must be brought back into the heart and pinned down there. It will struggle violently against capture and will be driven to defend itself by cunning rationalizations. But if the aspirant's own patience matches the ego's robust antagonism and if grace is sought and found, victory will come at last. So subtle an enemy on the path is the ego that even when the Overself's grace is leading us onward through our mystical practices to moments of sacred exaltation, the ego surreptitiously steals the credit for these results.

All the way from the quest's start to its finish the aspirant will need and must have the capacity for self-extinguishing humbleness and self-abasing reverence. The first is needed not in the presence of others, but of God; the second not in the bustle of the world, but in the secrecy of the heart. The lower ego must surrender to the higher individuality, not to another ego.

The need for a self-humbling before the Overself (which is not the same as self-humbling before others) is greatest of all with aspirants of an intellectual type. The veil of egotism must be lifted and with our own hands pride must be humbled to the dust. So long as we believe we are wise and meritorious for entertaining spiritual aspiration, so long will the Higher Self withhold the final means for realizing that aspiration. As soon as we believe we are foolish and sinful, the Higher Self will begin by its grace to help overcome these faults. Then when our humility extends until it becomes a realization of utter helplessness, the moment has come to couple it with intense prayer and ardent yearning for divine grace. And this humility toward the Higher Self must become as abiding an attitude as firmness toward the lower one. It must persist partly because we must continually realize that we need and will forever need its grace, and partly because we must continuously acknowledge our ignorance, folly, and sinfulness.

Thus the ego becomes convinced of its own unwisdom, and when it bends penitently before the feet of the Overself, it begins to manifest the wisdom that hitherto it lacked. Instead of wasting its time criticizing others, it capitalizes its time in criticizing itself. In old-fashioned theological language, we must consider ourselves unworthy sinners; then only do we become able to receive grace. We should measure our spiritual stature not by the lower standards of the conventional multitude, but by the loftier standards of the Ideal. The one may make us feel smug, but the other will make us feel small.

At some moments we may feel the animal within us, at other moments the criminal, and at rarer moments the angel. We must convict ourselves of sin, must become deeply aware of our wretched state in clinging so hard and so long to vanity, animality, selfishness, and materiality.

We may become anxious about our progress, disappointed about its slowness, or confused about its nature. But our striving must be patient and sustained, always faithful to its far-off goal, and we should not become blinded to the necessity for maintaining a balanced personality. Nor should we become so obsessed that every trivial fluctuation of feelings is regarded with exaggerated importance and studied with morbid analysis. In short, we must not become overanxious neurotics. The repeated dwelling upon our faults, the constant analysis of deficiencies, the self-exposure of missteps and mistakes should humble, chasten, and purify us.

The keeping of a diary devoted to confessing and noting faults in conduct and feeling as they appear may also be a help in the work of self-improvement.

Because we must first recognize and correct errors and sins, critical self-examination must not depend on itself alone but must also take guidance from the consequences of actions and the criticisms of enemies. Where the ordinary person sees only enmity, the earnest aspirant sees a chance to hasten growth. Where the one deplores opposition, the other uses it for his or her own development.

The ego is ever eager to defend itself by deceiving itself, ever gratified to cover its own shortcomings by pointing out those of other people, and seizing upon the wrong example set by others to rationalize its own wrong conduct.

Disciples cannot take the easy course of always blaming someone else's misdemeanors and never their own. What we know of our own self, with its defects and frailties and sinfulness, should teach us a little caution about others, a little carefulness in our dealings with them. We should be as silent about the faults of others as we should be eager to correct our own. Only where public or private duty make it imperative to speak out, or where we are actually asked for such criticism by the person concerned, need we break this rule.

We must liberate ourselves from emotional pride and intellectual self-conceit. The confession of our personal powerlessness is the first step to the discovery of our impersonal strength, and grace will begin to operate when we feel that we can no longer operate, no longer direct our own lives without falling into further sinfulness and further foolishness.

A person's ego is naturally unwilling to put itself obediently under the behest of the Overself. Only when it breaks down through the miserable results of its own mistakes and turns despairingly contrite through the sense of its own failures, does it begin to renounce this unwillingness.

To the extent that we empty ourselves of ourselves, to that extent the Overself may enter into our ordinary consciousness. But the displacement of the ego will not and cannot happen through any act of our own will. It will be produced in our emotional and intellectual consciousness by an act of the divine will.

Those who have the humility, strength, and wisdom to give their personal will back to the Higher Self thereby give the chance for forces greater than their own to bless, inspire, and use them. Let us have the courage to perform this one dynamic act of self-abnegation. We will never regret it. For whatever it takes from us, it will return more.

The simple meaning of those common mystical expressions—"self-annihilation," "giving up the ego," or "losing the 'I'"—is to put aside the thoughts, emotions, and personal affairs that ordinarily occupy the mind and to let the latter sink unhindered into a state of complete absorption in a felt higher power. It is a self-offering to the sublime entity within us.

Aspirants are told to displace the egotistic life only because they may thereby find a deeper and superior life. We are not to deny our existence, but to change its quality for the better. And the ego itself must prepare the way for this phenomenal change by forsaking its self-pride and by supplicating the Overself to possess it thoroughly.

The advice to look within would be idiotic if it meant only looking at the student's human frailty and mortal foolishness. But it really means looking further and deeper. It means an introspective examining operation much longer in time, much more exigent in patience, much more sustained in character than a mere first glance. It means intensity of the first order, concentration of the strongest kind, spiritual longing of the most fervent sort. We will need to look into our hearts more deeply than ever before, and search its darker labyrinths for the motives and desires hiding there from our conscious aspiration. We are called upon to make the most searching criticism of ourselves and to make it with emotional urgency and profound remorse.

So long as we are enslaved by our lower nature, so long will we be subject to confusions and misunderstandings, so long will we cherish delusions and deceptions during this period of our search for truth. Hence the need for an effort to transcend the lower nature through self-discipline. We start this inner work best with the firm understanding that we are sinful, faulty, and ignorant, and with humble realization of our personal unworthiness, our great need of self-improvement, purification, and ennoblement.

The aspirant should guard against allowing over-strong emotions or undisciplined passions to break down the maintenance of moral and mental balance. Even personal bitterness over a great injustice may harm it.

We do not say that philosophic students, as distinct from philosophical sages, should be entirely without passion. We only say these two things about it. First, we should strive to create a central core within which our passions cannot touch us, and whereby they are themselves controlled and disciplined—a level of profound remembrance where they suddenly lie still. Second, we should rescue them from being exclusively animal in character and redirect them to human channels also. Intellectual and artistic passions should be cultivated as a complement to those of a lower level.

If the inner life is repeatedly wasted by passion, we will know no assured peace and attain no enduring goal. We must govern ourselves, rule our passions, and discipline our emotions. We must strengthen our higher will at the expense of our lower one. For the first promotes our spiritual evolution whereas the second inflames our animal nature. We must present an imperturbable front to the inescapable ups and downs of life, and we must guard our hearts against becoming the sport of tumultuous emotions and riotous passions. Our emotional attitudes toward others must be watched lest we betray our deeply hidden invulnerable independence and suffer its loss in consequence.

The hardest task we can ever undertake is to align our lower ego with our Higher Self. This objective cannot be reached by feeble means. It demands all a person's powers and faculties and it demands them at peak level. It demands a wholesale and wholehearted reorientation of thought, ideal, and will. The enterprise of patching up the old way of life under the belief that we are setting up a new one is self-deceptive. If it is to have any karmic value, repentance must not end with emotion alone. The final proof of a changed heart is a changed life.

The result of this self-critical effort to remake the personality will be self-punishment. We will see the acute need to make reparation for former wrongdoing and, as we try to make it, this reparation will take two different forms. The first is where it involves others, and we will make our peace with them. The second is where it involves ourselves alone, and here we will perform penance and impose an ascetic discipline.

We must train to view thoughts in the proper perspective, refusing to regard their insistent attractions and repulsions as our own. We must cultivate the habit of being an observer of our own thoughts and activities in the same objective way as we observe strangers in the street. We must regard ourselves with detachment and experiences with calm, if we are to arrive at the truth of the one and learn the lessons of the other. While we cling to the possessive little ego, we cling also to fears and anxieties, discords and despair. We get too emotionally involved in our personal problems and so obscure true issues, or distort or magnify them.

If we have continued faithfully with our meditations and disciplines, our studies and aspirations, the time will come when we will approach a cyclic turn in our inner life, when we will review the pages of both our remote and recent past. During this turning point we will be tormented by grievous thoughts of our unworthy pasts and by consequent self-reproach. We will pass through a period of intense self-criticism. These sharp pains of conscience and bitter remorse are inevitable during this purificatory period when our past assumes an uglier configuration in the light that falls upon it, when we are first made aware of the dark places in our character and the weak parts of our nature.

Such memories will enter our minds unbidden. They will concern themselves only with the darker side, however, only with our sins, mistakes, errors of thought, judgment, and conduct, with wrongs done unwittingly or willfully to others. With these broodings will be linked poignant memories of and bitter regrets for the unnecessary sufferings brought upon ourselves as a consequence, as well as remorse for lapses from the path of goodness and wisdom. Such reflections and feelings will spread themselves out intermittently and fragmentarily over a period of several months or even a couple of years, but at the proper time the period will be brought to a sudden, unexpected, and abrupt end with a tremendous emotional upheaval. This is the second "mystical crisis" (the first being that which set our feet on the path's entrance). It continues for three days. During this time, many of the chief episodes, happenings, and decisions, stretching back to childhood, involving remorse and regret, are relived in a kind of cinema-film review in which we are both spectator and actor. At no time in this review should ill-will or angry resentment against other people concerned in it arise. If it does, and we permit it to remain, the crisis may end abruptly in failure to yield its benefits. These remembrances should fill our heart to overflowing with despair at our own wickedness, weakness, and foolishness. We will be driven by our inner conscience to impugn both our character and intelligence as they manifested during internal struggles and external problems. Toward or at the end of this three-day experience, we may even feel it is better to die than to continue such a worthless life. We will perceive quite clearly how different, how much better for ourselves and others, how much happier, how much more fruitful its course would have been had we decided and acted more wisely. This perception will bring us immense anguish through the comparison of what was with what might have been.

But with the coming of the fourth day all this self-reproach will leave. A strong and clear intuition will now address itself to us in more or less the following words: "Take to heart and keep in remembrance the lessons of the past, but let go of the past itself. Avoid these sins, get these weaknesses out of your character, improve your judgment, make what amends you can. But be done with the past, and be at peace about it henceforth. Today you begin a new and higher life." Thereupon a vast feeling of relief rises up within us and a welcome mood of peace enfolds us for some days.*

The pursuit of this Spiritual Self is not to be undertaken as a hobby, nor as an adjunct to eating and working. The task of changing ourselves is the greatest one any person can undertake. It is a lifetime's work. This improving of ourselves and advancing of humanity, of elevating our character and increasing understanding, will keep us busy until the very end of our term on earth. The philosophical life is neither easy nor lazy, and perhaps it is only the

---

*This mystical crisis is strikingly similar to the after-death review of earth life described in *The Wisdom of the Overself.*

exceptional person who will engage in the adventure. It is hard work altering many habit-patterns that, in the light of philosophic teaching, now seem unsatisfactory. But inasmuch as we have accepted this teaching, we cannot help but wish to conform our whole life to it. The task is tremendous but not impossible. It is not only theoretically conceivable but practically achievable, and it is to be made our primary activity whence all others take root and draw life.

The quest must become the center of our thinking and hence of our living. We must be quest-conscious and surrender completely to the philosophic ideal, becoming thereby seekers after truth. We feel now that the inward completion and full possession of ourselves must be sought and found if life is to be endurable; we know now that hitherto we have been groping blindly after it. Henceforth the quest must be a conscious and deliberate one. We must now pass from dream to reality, from the wish to find the Soul to its fulfillment. These truths must be proven within our own experience and not remain merely a concept in the mind. We must believe more in our own activity for salvation and less in reliance on some individual teacher.

Philosophy teaches a sublime moral code to be followed for the disciple's own good as well as the good of one's fellow humans. Whatever differences in metaphysical outlook and external practices there may be between us and others, philosophers abhor quarrels and love amity. We observe tolerance toward all others. Although there is no moral code that can be called an absolute one, all moral codes must condemn hatred if they are to be worth the name at all.

As a consequence of all these strivings and meditations, disciplines, and reflections, certain changes will take place in us. Little by little the mental images born of our lowest self fade out of consciousness, and we may come to see the whole of our past life as a dream. The sense of the Soul's nearness becomes real, and will become for us a daily presence and a continuous reality.

There comes with the traveling of this path a subordination of personal identity, a diminution of those egoistic limits that keep us from attaining our best in life, an abstraction from the entire set of mundane desires that normally compose life.

Such people are set apart from the mass by their aspirations and fine sincerity.

If humans have not attained, it is because they have not sought.

EIGHT

The Probations and Tests of the Aspirant

To MASTER DESIRES, to overcome passions, and to ennoble emotions: self-reform and self-purification are the first practical fruits of philosophy. Thus an interval of long probation must inevitably pass before the results of this effort can become apparent in thought and action. The task before us is really a tremendous one, requiring our whole nature and our best mind. Anything less will bring us so much nearer to failure. And its significance is so vast that failure will, in turn, bring a like measure of mental suffering. We may believe that we have already achieved certain things, but we should remember: first, the French proverb that the better is the enemy of the good; second, that whether our progress is genuine or whether, being so, it can maintain itself, is a matter that still needs to be ascertained. Our fidelity to the higher values and how far our spirituality is real or supposed, are sure to be put to appropriate tests at intervals of our mystical career. All our earlier experiences and preceding struggles, victories, and defeats have been a training for them. Hence we may expect temptations to accompany us at one period and tribulations at another. We hardly know what weaknesses are waiting beneath the surface of our conscious life, ready to rise above it when opportunity offers.

In some great mystery schools of antiquity, it was the task of the Grand Master to administer the necessary tests and arrange the fateful ordeals that determined the fitness of a candidate for entry into any of the successive degrees of initiation. The Egyptian hierophants applied their tests of the worthiness of candidates before granting them the enlightenment of initiation. The ordeals were divided into five ascending grades. Each corresponded to a different element—earth, water, air, fire, and spirit. Candidates for initiation into esoteric degrees were made by the hierophants to enter places that tried their nerves and to undergo ordeals that tested their courage. They also brought the candidates into surroundings and among individuals where powerful temptations to their sensual desires had to be overcome. But those schools have perished and their methods have perished with them. They would not indeed suit the conditions of the modern world.

The farther we advance, the more formidable and less recognizable will be the obstacles, trials, and temptations we will have to overcome. Men and women, circumstances and situations, will be used as bait to tempt us from the quest's moral ideals or disciplinary phases, from its intellectual goals and ideological truths. One of the strange methods used by the powers to test us will be to arrange coincidences in our external life-cycle. Thus, within a short time—sometimes within a single day of our solemn renunciation of a certain thing, it will be offered to us! Such coincidences may be evil or good. In the very moment when we are powerfully attracted by some desirable thing or person, we are to renounce it deliberately and heroically. In the very midst of a situation where the ego has but to stretch forth its hand and take, we are to practice self-abnegation discriminatingly and relentlessly. At such times, we may remember well the warning of Awhadi, a medieval Persian mystic: "When Fortune's cup into your hands doth pass, think of the headache as you raise the glass!"

These experiences are designed to make us conscious of the weaknesses in our character and to show how far we have really withdrawn from vanity, passion, ambition, and possessiveness. What we are in our deepest impulses will betray itself during our probation. These ordeals will be the final proving-ground for our character and will forcibly reveal its weaknesses and deficiencies. No concealment will be possible. Although the same opportunities, the same trials, and the same temptations cannot repeat themselves in precisely identical circumstances, nevertheless they may do so on levels of a different kind. For sins and faults seldom entirely disappear, but often recapitulate themselves in subtler ways or more refined forms. The chief latent weaknesses will be stimulated until they show themselves. This happens largely because the outer circumstances, in which they can express themselves freely, are now provided by fate. If we prove too weak to resist them, then the tragedy of a fall in consciousness will be enacted alongside our moral fall.

Some of these seeming opportunities present the most attractive appearances, behind which it will not be easy to discern what the reality really is. Satan sets traps at intervals along the path. They are so cunningly disguised that they look like pleasant parlors instead, and those who fall into them may spend years under the delusion that they are actually in a parlor. If the adverse forces cannot entrap us by blatant seductions, they will try to do so by subtle ones.

Refinement of feelings and elevation of ideas attained in our religious and mystical experiences have to be remembered whenever such temptations find a place to lodge. They will take the forms that they have always taken in humankind's long passage from enslavement by the flesh to exaltation by the Soul—the forms of sex and money, power and position, property and self-regard, and so on. But, in addition to these, there are some special forms peculiar to the mystical quest. They are ways of exploiting it for personal power, vanity, or profit. But the result of such action is continual self-contradiction. If we use the Soul as a lever to gain personal ends, we lose it. For it will not abide with anyone who loves it for less than itself. If we invite the higher forces to use us, we must not expect them to share us with the lower ones.

For instance, the notion of selling spiritual help for financial gain should, at any stage, be unthinkable. If we do so, then we will surely lose both knowledge and power through being cast down into the abyss. When we are sufficiently advanced, even the notion of accepting voluntarily offered contributions will become equally repellent. We may not know, at first, why this feeling comes to us, however, for it will come as a vague inner prompting. It is indeed a lead given by our Higher Self. If we fail to obey this prompting, then the Higher Self will, for a certain period, fail to reveal itself. We are to desire the Divine and assist its seekers for its own sake alone, not even for the mixed motives of securing both its inner presence and its outer rewards.

If spiritual help is to be given in the way it ought to be given—as an altruistic service—no payment should be taken, not even in the least obvious and most disguised form. No money gifts should be accepted, whether as remuneration for work done or as contribution to the work's cost. Indeed teachers must not only put students and seekers in their spiritual debt but also in their material debt. For if they undertake to go out and teach others, as far as they can they should pay the very traveling expenses incurred as a result of making the journey to reach them. It is highly undesirable to let either the mention of reward by the disciple, or the thought of it by the teacher, enter and sully the pure relationship between them. The only thing that they may rightly accept, should it be voluntarily offered and should they choose to do so, is hospitality while away from home—that is, shelter and food as a temporary guest.

These prohibitions may seem unduly rigorous, but if we consider what is likely to be gained by them they will then seem worthwhile. First, the students will receive a vivid demonstration and inspiring example of perfectly selfless service. Second, where teachers have not yet completely crushed their ego, they will avoid the risk of their motives losing their purity, their hearts losing non-attachment, and their lives losing independence. Any service that really helps others but that keeps up the server's ego may be good for them but is bad for the server. For the second object of rendering service is to lessen the ego's strength. Spiritual teachers, above all others, are expected by God and others to be the first to follow their own teachings and to practice the virtue that they inculcate. This is why it is a grave responsibility to appear before the world as such a one. Their doctrines must come out of their own experiences as well as thought, out of their own noble actions as well as elevated beliefs. Only egoless adepts have the right to receive money, for they alone can be trusted to use it for impersonal ends. But even they will rarely be willing to do so. Thus, two serious tests connected with money will have to be passed.

THE GLAMOR OF OCCULTISM

At some stage, practitioners of meditation are likely to have extraordinary experiences or develop powers of visionary, mediumistic, or hypnotic character. Our developed concentration will energize all our thoughts. As they increase in power, so should we increase in carefulness over them. Danger to others as well as to ourselves lurks here, but beneficence too. Those who fall victim to the lure of occult forces and let themselves become obsessed by thirst for their permanent possession, first get mentally confused, then lose their way altogether and desert the higher path, and finally fall into sheer black magic. If the worst happens, they will bring ethical ruin and material disaster upon themselves and those who become associated with them. The earnest aspirant should prefer to follow a lonely path rather than to follow the crowd that foolishly runs after the sensational, the occult, the psychic, the fanatic, and the pseudo-mystical, or joins esoteric cults.

One way in which the opposing power works to bring about the downfall of promising students is to influence them to believe, prematurely and incorrectly, that they stand in a highly advanced position. They are told flattering things about themselves to test their vanity. They are thus rendered overconfident and soon deceive first themselves and then others.

While we are dominated by the ego and its desires, we court the greatest dangers of, first, intellectually misunderstanding our experiences, and second, ethically misusing the powers in order to attain selfish ends at the cost, or even to the injury of other persons. In most cases, however, the Overself in its wisdom lets these occult powers lie in reserve until such time as the strength of egoism has sufficiently slackened, until moral power and philosophic knowledge have sufficiently manifested themselves within us to render their use safe to us and those with whom we have dealings. Only when it is no longer possible for us voluntarily to injure another person in any way for some selfish consideration, does the Higher Self deem us ready to possess such powers permanently.

There is, however, an unpredictable element in the pattern of human life, which increases rather than decreases as the quality of that life rises above the average. We see it markedly in the case of maturing aspirants who have to undergo tests and endure ordeals that have no karmic origin but which are put across their path by their own Higher Self for the purpose of a swifter forward-movement. They are intended to promote and not delay growth, to accelerate and not impede development. But they will achieve this purpose only if we recognize their true aim. Such recognition is impossible if we persist in clinging to the lower ego's standpoint or if, sensing the unearned character of this suffering, we treat them with resentment rather than with comprehension, with bitterness rather than with resignation. Thus human life is not wholly confined within the rigid bounds of karmic law. The Overself, which is after all its real essence, is free. We who have entered our name in this high enterprise of the quest must be prepared to trust our whole existence into its sacred hands, must be ready to accept and eager to understand the tribulations and afflictions that its deeper wisdom may see fit to impose upon us.

By a series of successive losses, troubles, or disappointments, or of so-called good fortune ending in these painful things, seekers will be successively parted from those attachments that they had not the strength to part from willingly. We have entered a stage where we are being assayed from within and without, where our yearnings and attachments, our virtues and vices, will be forced to show their real strength.

Let no one engage in the quest with the false hopes of a perpetual good time. For we have also engaged in a struggle. Once aspirants take to the quest, peace—in the sense of inward idleness or outward eventlessness—will never again be theirs. The relation between the lower and higher natures will always be one of tension and, at certain crises, this will be terrible and unbearable. Our preliminary struggles will deny us any smug rest or complacent satisfaction. Depressive moods will inevitably come again and again as we become poignantly aware of faults and shortcomings or filled with memories of lapses and failures. We have to overcome prejudices and conquer passions, to abandon the lower emotions and discipline the lower mind.

Hostile forces, open or disguised, will challenge us or will wait in ambush for us along the path. We will have to make our way between them. For they will employ baits to lure us from the quest, devise snares to entrap us, and use people to hurt us in various ways in fulfillment of maleficent designs. Suggestions will come to us that, if persistently traced to their source, despite their appearance of correctness, virtue, or wisdom, will be found to originate in such forces. The danger of losing our way besets us at every stage until we have emerged from completion of our novitiate. This situation exists equally for the aspirant who walks guideless and the one who walks with a trustworthy guide. No master can exempt us from the necessity of facing ordeals, experiencing temptations, undergoing trials, and being beset by the harassment of adverse forces.

The very last sentence uttered by the dying Buddha to his disciples contained the warning words: "Be on your guard." The farther we advance, the more we must be on our guard against the wiles of evil forces, whose operations to lead us astray grow subtler and subtler as we grow wiser and stronger. The harder we work, the more we provoke opposition; the swifter our travel, the more often we meet with temptations, snares, and traps. As novices, we will have to fight the promptings of such forces inside ourselves. For an adept, such forces will be driven out of lodgement in his or her mind and heart only to find lodgement in the minds and hearts of other men or women, who will thereupon become suddenly antagonistic to the adept. These persons may, in a few cases, belong to the adept's personal environment; in some cases they will be brought to cross his or her path; in others they will only have heard of the adept. But each will manifest some negative quality in response to demonistic suggestions and direct it against the adept. There will be a mesmeric character about each suggestion. It may be doubt, suggestion, lying, anger, fear, envy, or hatred. There will be attempts to embitter feelings, inflame passion, and arouse hatred. This adverse power seeks to hinder or even destroy the aspirant's personal progress as it seeks to hinder or destroy an adept's altruistic endeavors to promote the progress of humankind. The latter, especially, may suffer criticism, endure unearned vilification, or experience spiteful opposition too.

Thus when inner troubles are at last overcome, outer troubles begin to rear their heads. We may avoid the first by avoiding the quest. We may escape the second by renouncing altruism and becoming self-centered mystics. This is why philosophy is for the strong and compassionate only, not for cowards, egotists, or idlers. Nevertheless adeptship has it compensations. If others here stumble in the night or grope through the dusk, the adept walks surefootedly in clear noonday light. And where they must struggle alone, the adept on the contrary is ever conscious of a blessed presence at his or her side.

Persons expressing negative forces are nothing less than mental highwaymen and will one day suffer the karmic penalty for such wrongdoing. It is easy for the discerning to recognize the unmistakable marks of false or unscrupulous pretension when they appear as extreme and exaggerated personal claims—as the cloven hoof of commercialistic exploitation, as the incitement to sexual looseness, as the suave encouragement of political hate and social destructiveness—but it is difficult for the unsophisticated to recognize them when they are masked by lofty teachings or fine phrases.

THE DANGER OF OBSESSION

The next danger that the disciple has either to foresee and avoid or to meet and overcome, is that of becoming partially influenced or intermittently obsessed by an evil spirit who has emerged from the darkness of tellurian depths. This danger arises from our ignorance of the psychic forces and their mode of operation, from the moral impurities and emotional indiscipline of our character, and, above all, from our increased sensitivity, from our inescapable necessity of cultivating a passive, surrendered attitude, and from wrong meditation causing mystical development to degenerate into a merely mediumistic development. Just as there are divine invasions of our inner psychological being when grace sheds its light upon us, so there may also be demonic invasions when we go astray from the path. That the will of a disincarnate being may control the body of an incarnate one is one of those abnormal possibilities that we must admit into our scheme of things. That this will is more often evil than good is, unfortunately, quite true. That demonistic possession is in short a psychological fact, and not merely an exploded superstition, is a warning whose utterance is necessary.

The possibility of evil spirits usurping the human ego's rightful place is real. It is a possibility that was recognized by antique races throughout the world and still is recognized in most Eastern lands. It is satisfying to know that, in the kingdoms of Nature, this race of invisible demons is kept apart from the race of human beings by a strong psychic wall. But it is disturbing to learn that under abnormal conditions they may break through this wall. Unhappy sufferers' willpower may be completely overcome, their bodily organs completely used, and their mental faculties completely overshadowed by the supplanting entity at certain times—mostly during the hours of darkness. When a malevolent entity possesses them, when an unseen evil influence overshadows their mind, they feel that they are performing actions not dictated by their own personality. The unfortunate victims may or may not be conscious of what they are doing during the hours of obsession. If they are, their movements will be merely mechanical. If they are not, this will not prevent them from carrying on conversations with other persons.

It is a common trick with these invisible evil entities to secure the faith and trust of humans by cunning flattery, fulfilled predictions, or lofty teachings and, this done, to lead their unsuspecting feet over a precipice into material disaster, mental despair, and sometimes moral ruin. They conceal their real character at first, and may pretend to have the same moral ideals and religious beliefs as the person they are seeking to enslave. We may rightly suspect their presence when we feel the urge to make vital decisions in great external haste and under great internal pressure.

Anyone who has fallen into this danger of obsession will best be liberated from it by the help of a mystical adept or a true priest. Sometimes a single interview will suffice to effect the liberation. The exorciser will probably have to perform a short external rite in addition to internal mental work. Where such help is not procurable, sufferers may attempt to perform the rite of exorcism themselves. It begins with kneeling down in humble prayer for help, protection, or salvation to whatever higher power or inspired master they have most faith in. It ends with the firm utterance: "I command you in the name, by the power and compassion of X–, to come out of this body," combined with the sign of the cross made positively and slowly with the right forefinger. On a deep inhaled breath, the same sign is to be made again, simultaneously with the same utterance repeated silently and mentally only. "X–" represents the name of any higher power or personage in whom there is full faith. This rite should be performed each morning and each night before retiring to bed.

FALLS ON THE PATH

The way is not a smooth, untroubled movement from one satisfying position to another. It is a to-and-fro struggle, an incessant fight, a mixture of victories and defeats. Therefore it should not be a matter for surprise that so many candidates fail to pass these tests and abandon the quest in its early or intermediate stages. But even after successfully passing them, there arises the further danger of falling from whatever height has been attained, which is another peril to be guarded against by novices, intermediates, and even proficients—in fact by all who have not yet reached the final degree. Until this degree is reached it is always possible for aspirants to slip from their positions and fall back. The risk is even greater for the proficient than for the neophyte for, in the degree before the last one, the occult opposition to progress rises to its crescendo; the temptations become more subtle, more numerous, and more complex than ever before. In this grade, we have arrived close to success, but that is the very reason why we must guard our gains with the utmost vigilance. Otherwise, through the machinations of evil forces, we may unwittingly cast them all away. Having reached this penultimate stage, we have reached the position of one who, though in sight of the harbor, may still be shipwrecked. It is then, more than ever before, that the adverse forces will make their last desperate attempts to detain, overcome, or destroy us, to plunge us into unutterable despair or moral ruin. We must beware of diabolically inspired efforts to deprive us of all that we have gained and will need to take the utmost care to protect and conserve it. During this phase, we must test our foothold at every step as we take it, moving with the utmost care and ensuring the fullest safeguard. All our shrewdness and sincerity, all our discrimination and patience must be drawn upon to surmount this ordeal triumphantly.

Other tests will come, both to intermediates and proficients, through the egoistic emotions being awakened as a subsequent reaction to ecstatic mystical experience or by the discovery that subtle mental powers are developing within as a fruit of that experience.

Our path will be staged by pseudo-attainments, which may bear some but never all the marks of the true, final attainment. If the experience is of the right kind, we will feel no inflated pride in having had it; rather, we will feel a greater humility than before, knowing how dependent it is on the Overself's grace. Indeed it is better that we should not communicate it to others, but remain silent about what is happening to our inner life. And this is sound counsel for other reasons, too. For if through ardent longing or mere vanity we allow ourselves to fall into deception about our true spiritual status, and especially if the experience be used as justification for setting up as a public teacher or cult-founder, then the "dark night of the soul" will descend on us, too.

We should wait patiently until the divine assurance clearly and unmistakably comes that it is within our competence to engage in such activity. Until then we should beware lest our emotions be carried away, not by the divine impulsion but by our own egotism. We should not interfere with the self-chosen spiritual paths of others. Yet what may be wrong for us, at our present stage, may in later years be permissible if we reach a higher one. For then we will speak out of wisdom and not out of foolishness; we will act out of impersonality and not out of the limited ego.

To remain faithful to the teaching when passing through a test or an ordeal becomes easier when we realize that this is what the experience really is. We will be tested not only for sincere loyalty to ideals but also for adequate comprehension of ideas. If we find ourselves confused and unclear, this will be a pointer to new channels for our study. Should we desert the quest, circumstances will so shape themselves and repentances will so persistingly intrude themselves that, whether within a few years or half a lifetime, we will have to yield to the call or else suffer the penalty, which is to be struck down in premature death or life-wasting madness by our Higher Self.

We need to be intellectually prepared and emotionally purified before the Higher Self will descend to enlighten intellect and ennoble emotion. Hence, before it sheds the sunshine of grace upon our way, it will test our perseverance in this effort and try our faith to a point of anguish, which at times seems beyond endurance. In the moods of black despair that will inevitably follow each failure, we may dwell again and again on the thought of abandoning the quest altogether. Yet, if we hold on, an end will come and rich reward with it. If always we return to the right path in a humble, chastened, and repentant mood, we will be given the needful help to redeem our past and safeguard our future. Grace is ever ready to mantle its *shekinah* (Divine presence, or Holy Spirit), in protection, over the truly penitent.

All these and other tests are in the end calls to greater and greater self-purification. When our yearnings for the Spirit are thoroughly permeated with ardor and passion and when these qualities are deep and sustained, it will greatly help to achieve hard renunciations and surmount temptations. But it comes to this in the end— that all lesser loves have necessarily to be thrust out of the heart to make room for the supreme love that it inexorably demands from us. There is little virtue in surrendering what means nothing to us, only in surrendering what means everything to us. Consequently the test will touch our hearts at the tenderest points. Will we step out of our little ringed-in circle of personal loves, desires, and attachments, into the infinite, unbounded ocean of impersonal love, self-sufficiency, satisfaction, and utter freedom?

The choice is a hard one only so long as we keep our gaze fastened on the first alternative and remain ignorant of all that the second one really means. For whatever delight the first can possibly yield us, that delight is already contained in the second. But it is contained merely as a watery dilution of the grandly ineffable consciousness that the

Real offers us. We should be wise or experienced enough to comprehend now that if each attachment gives the pleasure of possession, it also gives the disappointment of limitation. The one cannot be had without the other. Every egoistic feeling that stands in the way of our utter self-giving to the Spirit, every personal bond that inhibits our fullest self-surrender to it, must go. But the agony of our loss is soon overwhelmed by the joy of our gain. The sacrifice that is asked from us turns out to be compensated for on a higher level with immensely richer treasure.

This does not mean that we need abandon the lesser loves altogether or crush them completely. It means that we are to give them second place, that they are to be guided and governed by the Soul.

Tests are a necessary part of spiritual growth. When we can be placed among desirable possessions or foods or people and feel no temptation to reach out for what is not proper or right or intemperate for us, we can be regarded as being masters of ourselves.

We are seeking truth. The opposite of truth is falsehood. Therefore, these forces seek to divert us into thoughts, feelings, and deeds that will falsify our quest. Hence the warning given in Plato's precepts to Aristotle, "Be always on the alert, for malignancy works in manifold disguises."

There are snares cruelly laid to entrap us, deceptions cunningly fashioned to lead us astray, and pitfalls callously dug to destroy us. Nor are these all to be met with in our external fortunes only. They occur inside our own fortress also. Our own intellect, emotions, impulses, and character may betray us into the hands of these adverse forces. If a disciple falls victim to a temptation, makes a wrong decision, becomes deluded by a false teacher, or is misled by a false doctrine, this can happen only if there exists some inner weakness in the character or intelligence that responds to these outer causes. If we may lay blame upon them for the unfortunate result, we must lay much more blame upon ourselves. The "dark night of the soul" that may then follow is a warning from our Higher Self to practice penetrative self-scrutiny, to ferret out this weakness, and to set about its gradual elimination.

Thus aspirants will find themselves engaged in a war against evil forces. Their metaphysical existence being granted, their practical helpfulness in discovering and exposing our weaknesses must also be granted. Nevertheless the need to defend ourselves against them still arises. It is for us to see that we so conduct ourselves in thought and deed as to frustrate their dangerous machinations. But the first protection against them is, as already mentioned, always to regard the lower ego as our worst enemy. For it is the smug repository of all our failings, weaknesses, and wickednesses—the unguarded door through which those who dislike, oppose, or hate us may really cause us harm. It is highly important, for this and several other reasons, for every serious student of philosophy to make the sacrifice of the self-love and self-worship that bolster up these weaknesses and defend them against all accusations. So long as we persist in maintaining an inner acceptance of their right to exist, so long will we be unable to climb out of the pit of darkness where we dwell with the rest of humankind and also to keep these unseen forces in permanent defeat.

Purity of motive in our dealings with others and loftiness of character in our thoughts of them, are further requisites. These too will protect us from some of the perils to which we are exposed, but not from all.

If we are to escape from this twilight realm of empty fancies and distorted realities, we must devote ourselves to purifying the body, emotions, and mind, to developing the reason and strengthening the will. This will provide us with the needed means of obliterating vain illusions and correcting disordered perceptions.

Psychic manifestations may be vouchsafed to us, but the question of their degree of authenticity will remain, whether or not we like to look it in the face. Until we have reached the firm ground of sufficient knowledge, purity, balance, and critical judgment, we would be wiser not to seek and pursue such manifestations.

Too many are carried away by a current of sensational psychic messages and experiences that makes its beginning nowhere but in the fantasies of their own subconscious mind. Here the imagination is released and left without control, as in the dream-state, so that anything may happen and anyone may be encountered. The wish to be personally honored by the association and guidance of a famous or exotic master finds here its imaginative realization. In this way, self-hallucination easily starts to rule their lives.

Those who become preoccupied with such messages, whose belief in them and their importance is unlimited, tend to stray from the real quest—which should be for the Overself alone and not for the occult phenomena incidental to it. If the messages are falsely imagined, they fall into the danger of attributing to a higher being what is actually their own subconscious creation.

We will be brought into brief contact or long association with the persons or ideas, with the examples or atmospheres of others who may unwittingly be used to bring out more fully the latent or half-expressed traits of our character. According to their own natures, they will either provoke the evil or influence the good to manifest itself. Once humble, we may begin to become arrogant. Or, once clean-living, we may begin to become dissolute.

When aspirants are about to take a wrong course, the result of which will be suffering, they will receive warning either from within by intuition or from without through some other person. In both cases, its source will be their Higher Self.

Vanity pursues both fledgling aspirants and matured proficients with its flattering whisper. Even at the threshold of the divinest attainments, there comes the ambition to found a new religion where they will be held in superstitious reverence, start their own sect of easily led followers, or acquire an adoring flock of disciples within a school or ashram. Of course, the temptation disguises itself as an act of altruistic service. But such service can safely and rightly begin only when the ego's dominance has utterly and permanently gone and the personal inadequacies have been remedied. A premature yielding to this masked temptation will inevitably bring down the misery of a "dark night" upon them. Personal ambitions very easily dress themselves in the peacock feathers of service to humanity. Those who wish to serve their generation must equip and prepare themselves for such service, must purify, enlighten, and develop their inner being. Only as they become strong in themselves can they inspire strength in those who come within range of their personal influence. Their egos must first become instruments in holy hands, servants of sacred commands.

There is one special value of these experiences, tests, or ordeals that often makes them of front-rank importance. What disciples cannot achieve through mental self-training, except after several years of time, they may achieve in a few days of reacting in an unwonted but right way to such tests. Because a decision or an action called for may be momentous in its nature and far-reaching in its consequences, if they leap bravely from a lower to a higher standpoint, from a selfish or desire-filled one to an altruistic or purer one, their spiritual advancements may be tremendously accelerated.

Whatever happens during the quest's long and varied course, it is always required of aspirants that we should never abandon faith in the divine power. It has brought people out of the gravest danger to perfect safety, out of hopeless situations to happier ones, out of disheartening stagnation to encouraging advancement. Setbacks will occur. They may weaken our efforts to find reality, but we should never let them weaken our faith in reality. During the tremendous and sometimes terrible vicissitudes of the years devoted to the mystical researches, what will sustain us throughout and, in the end, probably save us from utter destruction, will be faith and hope. Yet a faith that is unchecked and uncritical, a hope that is vain and deceptive can just as easily lead us straight into the dark fate. No! It is a faith in the Spirit rather than in others, a hope that places its value above all else, which will prove so effectual. We must hold its realization ever before us as a master aim to be patiently and perseveringly sought.

There cannot be an effective substitute for keenness of discernment. As we advance in the quest, we will need to develop the capacity to discern friends from foes, to peer under masks and to strip events of their appearances; otherwise, we will be entrapped, waylaid, or ambushed by evil forces whose pernicious business is often to disguise their maleficent operations under virtuous masks. Consequently it must be part of our business to be on our guard to penetrate behind their appearances. If it is the task of these forces to seduce us from the straight and narrow path, it is our task to discern their hand behind each attempt and to resist it. If we are to overcome them, it will not be enough to depend on our self-criticism, sincerity, and prayers, our nobility and goodness. We need to be informed about the existence of these forces, the signs whereby they may be recognized, the subtlety of their operations, the deceitfulness of their character, and the way they attack and lay ambushes. It is not only faith and hope that sustain us during these hard trials, but also intelligence and will, shrewdness, critical judgment, reasoning power, and prudence in dealing with these probationary tests and evil oppositions.

When Jesus said, "Except ye become as a little child, ye shall not enter the kingdom of heaven," he did not invite his hearers to become childish, foolish, or fanciful. Indeed, a warning is needful here. The mystic who forgets the complementary warning, "Be ye as shrewd as serpents," and who persists in misinterpreting Jesus's words as being an instruction to become irresponsible, gullible, and utterly uncritical, who believes that such qualities can bring us nearer to divine wisdom, is welcome to do so. This very belief makes one unfit to grasp the truth about the matter. But those who can fathom the philosophic meaning of the quotation know it to be an utterance of the highest importance. Students of philosophy who have trained themselves to look beneath the surface of things and to understand words with their heads as well as their hearts, regard it as being significant on three levels. First, it is an invitation to note that, just as a child surrenders its own self-reliance to what it regards as a higher being—its mother—so should the disciple surrender egoism to God and adopt that surrendered attitude, which is true humility. Second, it is a call to seek truth with a fresh mind, an unselfish mood, and a freedom from conventional preconceptions. Third, it is a warning that the natural goodness and purity, which make children so contrasting to adults, must be attained before the mystical consciousness can be attained. There is abundant evidence to corroborate this interpretation of Jesus's saying.

NINE

The Working of Grace

*On the day of life's surrender I shall die desiring Thee; I
shall yield my spirit craving of Thy street the dust to be.*

HUSAMUDDIN, FOURTEENTH-CENTURY
PERSIAN MYSTIC

IN THESE POETIC LINES is expressed the lengths to which the mystic must be willing to go to obtain grace.

Only those who fall in love with their Soul as deeply as they have
ever done with another will stand a chance of finding it. Incessant
yearning for the Higher Self, in a spirit of religious devotion, is one of
the indispensable aspects of the fourfold integral quest. The note of
yearning for this realization must sound through all our prayers and
worship, concentration and meditation. Sometimes the longing for
God may affect us even physically with abrupt dynamic force, shak-
ing our whole body, and agitating our whole nervous system. A merely
formal practice of meditation is quite insufficient although not quite
useless. For without the yearning the advent of grace is unlikely, and
without grace there can never be any realization of the Overself.

The very fact that we have consciously begun the quest is itself a manifestation of grace, for we have begun to seek the Overself only because the Overself's own working has begun to make it plain to us, through the sense of unbearable separation from it, that the right moment for this has arrived. The aspirant should therefore take heart and feel hope. We are not really walking alone. The very love that has awakened within us for the Overself is a reflection of the love that is being shown toward us.

Thus the very search upon which we have embarked, the studies we are making, and the meditations we are practicing are all inspired by the Overself from the beginning and sustained by it to the end. The Overself is already at work even before we begin to seek it. Indeed we have taken to the quest in unconscious obedience to the divine prompting. And that prompting is the first movement of grace. Even when we believe that we are doing these things for ourselves, it is really grace that is opening the heart and enlightening the mind from behind the scenes.

Our initiative pushes on toward the goal, while divine grace draws us to it. Both forces must combine if the process is to be completed and crowned with success. Yet that which originally made the goal attractive to us and inspired us with faith in it and thus gave rise to our efforts, was itself the grace. In this sense Paul's words, "For by Grace are ye saved through faith, and that not of yourselves," become more intelligible.

The grace of God is no respecter of persons or places. It comes to the heart that *desires it most* whether that heart be in the body of a king or of a commoner, a person of action or a recluse. John Bunyan, the poor tinker immured in Bedford gaol, saw a light denied to many kings and tried to write it down in his book, *Pilgrim's Progress*. Jacob Boehme, working at his cobbler's bench in Seidenberg, was thrice illumined, and gleaned secrets that he claimed were unknown to the universities of his time.

If we have conscientiously followed this fourfold path, if we have practiced mystical meditation and metaphysical reflection, purification of character and unselfish service, and yet seem to be remote from the goal, what are we to do? We have then to follow the admonition of Jesus: "Ask and ye shall receive, knock and it shall be opened unto you." We have literally to ask for grace out of the deep anguish of our hearts. We are all poor. We are indeed discerning, we who realize this and become beggars, imploring God for grace.

We must pray first to be liberated from the heavy thralldom of the senses, the desires, and the thoughts. We must pray next for the conscious presence of the Overself. We should pray silently and deeply in the solitude of our own hearts. We should pray with concentrated emotion and tight-held mind. Our yearning for such liberation and such presence must be unquestionably sincere and unquestionably strong. We should begin and close—and even fill if we wish—our hour of meditation with such noble prayers. We must do this day after day, week after week. For the Overself is not merely a concept, but a living reality, the power behind all our other and lesser powers.

No aspirant who is sincere and sensitive will be left entirely without help. It may appear during temptation when the lower nature may find itself unexpectedly curbed by a powerful idea working strongly against it. We may find in a book just that for which we have been waiting and which at this particular time will definitely help us on our way. The particular help we need at a particular stage will come naturally. It may take the form of a change in outward circumstances or a meeting with a more developed person, of a printed book or a written letter, of a sudden unexpected emotional inspiration or an illuminating intellectual intuition. Nor is it necessary to travel to the farthest point before being able to gather the fruits. Long before this, we will begin to enjoy the flavor of peace, hope, knowledge, and divine transcendence.

In the moment that we willingly desert our habitual standpoints under a trying situation and substitute this higher one, in that moment we receive grace. With this reception a miracle is performed and the evil of the lower standpoint is permanently expelled from our character. The situation itself both put us to the proof and gave us a chance.

The factuality of grace does not cancel out the need for moral choice and personal effort. It would be a great mistake to stamp human effort as useless in the quest and to proclaim human inability to achieve our own salvation as complete. For if it is true that Divine Grace alone can bring the quest to a successful terminus, it is likewise true that human effort must precede and thus invoke the descent of grace. What is needed to call down grace is: first, a humility that is utter and complete, deeply earnest and absolutely sincere; secondly, an offering of self to the Overself, a dedication of earthly being to spiritual essence; and, thirdly, a daily practice of devotional exercise. The practices will eventually yield experiences; the aspirations will eventually bring assistance. The mysterious intrusion of grace may change the course of events. It introduces new possibilities, a different current of destiny.

Our need of salvation, of overcoming the inherently sinful and ignorant nature of ego, isolated from true consciousness as it is, is greater than we ever comprehend. For our life, being so largely egotistic, is ignorant and sinful—a wandering from one blunder to another, one sin to another. This salvation is by the Overself's saving power, for which we must seek its grace, approaching it with the childlike humility of which Jesus spoke. No one is so down, so sinful, so weak, or so beaten that he or she may not make a fresh start. Let us adopt a childlike attitude, placing ourselves in the hands of our Higher Self, imploring it for guidance and grace. We should repeat this at least daily, and even oftener. Then let us patiently wait and carefully watch for the intuitive response during the course of the following weeks or months. We need not mind our faults. Let us offer ourselves, just as we are, to the God, or Soul, we seek. It is not indifferent nor remote.

The forgiveness of sins is a fact. Those who deny this deny their own experience. Can they separate from the moon its light? Then how can they separate forgiveness from love? Do they not see a mother forgive her child a hundred times even though she reproves and chastises it?

If the retribution of sins is a cosmic law, so also is the remission of sins. We must take the two at once, and together, if we would understand the mystery aright.

We humans are fallible beings prone to commit errors. If we do not become penitents and break with our past, it is better that we should be left to the natural consequences of our wrong-doing than that we should be forgiven prematurely.

The value of repentance is that it is the first step to set us free from a regrettable past; the value of amendment is that it is the last step to do so. There must be a contrite consciousness that to live in ego is to live in ignorance and sin. This sin is not the breaking of social conventions. There must be penitent understanding that we are born in sin because we are born in ego and hence need redemption and salvation. It is useless to seek forgiveness without first being thoroughly repentant. There must also be an opening up of the mind to the truth about one's sinfulness; besides repentance there must be an understanding of the lesson behind this particular experience of its result.

When St. Paul speaks in his Epistle to the Hebrews of the Christ who offered to bear the sins of many, he may be mystically interpreted as meaning the Christ Self, the Overself, who offers to bear the karma of many ego-incarnations.

This primary attribute is extolled in the world's religio-mystical literature. "Despair not of Allah's mercy," says the Koran. "What are my sins compared with Thy mercy? They are but as a cobweb before the wind," wrote an early Russian mystic, Dmitri of Rostov. "Those who surrender to me, even be they of sinful nature, shall understand the highest path," says the Bhagavad Gita.

Yes, there is forgiveness because there is God's love. Jesus was not mistaken when he preached this doctrine, but it is not a fact for all alike. Profound penitence and sincere amendment are prerequisite conditions to calling it forth. It was one of the special tasks of Jesus to make known that compassion (or *love,* as the original word was translated) is a primary attribute of God and that grace, pardon, and redemption are consequently primary features of God's active relation to humans. When Jesus promised the repentant thief that he would be forgiven, Jesus was not deceiving the thief or deluding himself. He was telling the truth.

The Divine being what it is, how could it contradict its own nature if compassion had no place in its qualities? The connection between the benignity that every mystic feels in its presence and the compassion that Jesus ascribed to that presence, is organic and inseparable.

The discovery that the forgiveness of sins is a sacred fact should fill us with inexpressible joy. For it is the discovery that there is compassionate love at the heart of the universe.

We may suppress sins by personal effort but we can eradicate and overcome them by the Overself's grace alone. If we ask only that the external results of our sin be forgiven, be sure they won't. But if we also strive to cleanse our character from the internal evil that caused the sin, forgiveness may well be ours.

The aspirant's best hope lies in repentance. But if we fail to recognize this, if we remain with unbowed head and unregenerate heart, the way forward will likewise remain stony and painful. The admission that we are fallible and weak will be wrung from us by the punishments of nature if we will not yield it by the perceptions of conscience. The first value of repentance is that it makes a break with an outworn past. The second value is that it opens the way to a fresh start. Past mistakes cannot be erased but future ones can be avoided. The person that we were must fill us with regret, the person that we seek to be, with hope. We must become keenly conscious of our own sinfulness. The clumsy handiwork of our spiritual adolescence will appall us whenever we meditate upon its defects. Our thought must distrust and purge itself of these faults. We will at certain periods feel impelled to reproach ourselves for faults shown, wrongs done, and sins committed during the past. This impulse should be obeyed. Our attitude must so change that we are not merely ready but even eager to undo the wrongs that we have done and to make restitution for the harm that we have caused.

We do not get at the Real by our own efforts alone nor does it come to us by its own volition alone. Effort that springs from the self and grace that springs from beyond it are two things essential to success in this quest. The first we can all provide, but the second only the Overself can provide. Humankind was once told by someone who knew, "The Spirit bloweth where it listeth." Thus it is neither contradictory nor antithetic to say that human effort and human dependence upon divine grace are both needed. For there is a kind of reciprocal action between them. This reciprocal working of grace is a beautiful fact. The subconscious invitation from the Overself begets the conscious invocation of it as an automatic response. When the ego feels attracted toward its sacred source, there is an equivalent attraction on the Overself's part toward the ego itself. Never doubt that the Divine always reciprocates this attraction to it of the human self. Neither the latter's past history nor present character can alter that blessed hope-bringing fact. Grace is the final, glorious, and authentic proof that it is not only we that are seeking God, but also God that is ever waiting for us.

Grace is a heavenly superhuman gift. Those who have never felt it and consequently rush into incautious denial of its existence are to be pitied. Those who flout the possibility and deny the need of a helping grace can be only those who have become victims of a cast-iron intellectual system that could not consistently give a place to it.

It was a flaming experience of grace that changed Saul, the bitter opponent, into Paul, the ardent apostle.

This is the paradox: although we must try to conquer ourselves if we would attain the Overself, we cannot succeed in this undertaking except by the Overself's own power—that is, by the grace "which burns the straw of desires," as Maha Upanishad poetically puts it. It is certain that such an attainment is beyond our ordinary strength.

All that the ego can do is to create the necessary conditions out of which enlightenment generally arises, but it cannot create this enlightenment itself. By self-purification, by constant aspiration, by regular meditation, by profound study, and by an altruistic attitude in practical life, it does what is prerequisite. But all this is like tapping at the door of the Overself. Only the latter's grace can open it in the end.

The will has its part in this process, but it is not the only part. Sooner or later we will discover that we can go forward no further solely depending on the will, and that we must seek help from something beyond ourselves. We must indeed call for grace to act upon us. The need of obtaining help from outside our ordinary self and from beyond our ordinary resources in this tremendous struggle becomes urgent. It is indeed a need of grace. Fortunately for us this grace is available, although it may not be so on our own terms.

At a certain stage we must learn to "let go" more and allow

the Overself to possess us, rather than strain to possess something that we believe to be still eluding us. Aspirants who have passed this stage will remember how they leapt ahead when they made this discovery.

At another stage, the Overself, whose grace was the initial impetus to all our efforts, steps forward, as it were, and begins to reveal its presence and working more openly. The aspirant becomes conscious of this with awe, reverence, and thankfulness. We must learn to attend vigilantly to these inward promptings of divine grace. They are like sunbeams that fructify the earth.

With the descent of grace, all the anguish and ugly memories of the seeker's past and the frustrations of the present are miraculously sponged out by the Overself's unseen and healing hand. We know that a new element has entered into our field of consciousness, and we will unmistakably feel from that moment a blessed quickening of inner life. When our own personal effort subsides, a further effort begins on our behalf by a higher power. Without any move on our own part, grace begins to do for us what we could not do for ourselves, and under its beneficent operation we will find our higher will strengthening, our moral attitude improving, and our spiritual aspiration increasing.

The consciousness of being under the control of a higher influence will become unmistakable to us. The conviction that it is achieving moral victories for us, which we could not have achieved by our ordinary self, will become implanted in us. A series of remarkable experiences will confirm the fact that some beneficent power has invaded our personality and is ennobling, elevating, inspiring, and guiding it. An exultant freedom takes possession of us. It displaces all our emotional forebodings and personal burdens.

Grace is received, not achieved. We must be willing to let its influx move freely through our hearts; we must not obstruct its working nor impede its ruling by any break in our own self-surrender. We can possess grace only when we let it possess us.

Philosophy affirms the existence of grace, that what the most strenuous self-activity cannot gain may be put in our hands as a divine gift.

As at the beginning, so at the end of this path, the unveiling of the Overself is not an act of any human will. Only the divine will—that is, only its own grace—can bring about the final all-revealing act, whose sustained consciousness turns the aspirant into an adept.

In seeking the Overself, the earnest aspirant must seek it with heartfelt love. Indeed, our whole quest must be ardently imbued with this feeling. Can we love the Divine purely and disinterestedly for its own sake? This is the question we must ask ourselves. If this devotional love is to be something more than frothy feeling, it will have to affect and redeem the will. It will have to heighten the sense of, and obedience to, moral duty. Because of this devotion to something that transcends our selfish interests, we can no longer seek our selfish advantage at the expense of others. Our aim will be not only to love the Soul but to understand it, not only to hear its voice in meditation but to live out its promptings in action.

TEN

Insight

IF REALITY EXISTS anywhere it must exist in an irreducible infinitude. But such a character places it beyond ordinary finite perceptions. A transcendental insight is therefore needful to bring us into relation with it. When the Supreme Reality is declared to be unknowable and unthinkable, we mean that it is unknowable only to physical sense perception and unthinkable only by intellectual consciousness. Although the Absolute is beyond our ordinary means of comprehension it is not beyond our extraordinary means. For there is in us a faculty that we may unfold that is higher than our ordinary means of comprehension: it is the faculty of transcendental insight, which can enable us to know and to experience this reality. The quest consummates itself in the philosophic experience, which is this unbroken enduring insight into the inner reality.

We discover ourselves as bodies through the eyes but discover ourselves as the Overself through insight. Thus, when experience has developed and perfected its own fullest self-comprehension, it has developed the instrument of insight. When we are so mesmerized by our personalities that we regard the Overself as non-existent and so mesmerized by the world-appearance that we regard Mind as a mere illusion, we are said to be dwelling in ignorance. When, however, we are aware of reality as intimately as we are aware of our own bodies, then only have we authentic insight. Our struggle to attain an understanding of life will not be brought to a decisive issue before insight has fully flowered.

This faculty must not be confused with a merely intellectual, one-sided, so-called insight. For the whole of our being shares in its operations, as the whole of our feeling-nature is penetrated by it. Whoever possesses this understanding possesses inextinguishable light. When reason can conquer its one-sidedness and admit the play of other elements, it will itself be absorbed in the higher and richer all-embracing faculty of immediate insight. In one sense insight is a synthetic faculty, for it blends the abstract reason of the metaphysician, the feeling of the artist, the intuition of the mystic, the concrete reason of the scientist, and the practical will of the active person. It fuses all these and yet it is also something higher, which transcends them all. What the metaphysician only recognizes intellectually and what the mystic only feels emotionally are contained, combined, and yet transcended in the philosophical insight.

Nor should it be confounded with intuition, of which it is the higher octave. Nor is it to be confused with mere clairvoyant vision.

Insight is a three-in-one faculty: it sees, it knows, and it is, all at the same time. Because knowing involves a duality of knower and known, it disappears at this point and merges into being. Realization is not a personal experience, for there is nothing personal in the Real. Nor does it consist of an intellectual activity, although the pressure of right intellectual activity is one of the factors that helps us to arrive at it. Its decree is alone authentic. Those who have this sure insight are liberated from the dogmas of ecclesiastics and the speculations of theologians, as well as from the aberrations of mystics and the imaginations of visionaries. Once we have attained to this higher consciousness, our worldview will possess a certitude superior even to that of mathematicians.

How can we be assured of the truth of insight? By the disappearance of ignorance, its opposite number. The two cannot coexist. Its truth is not an argument but an achievement. The coming of insight means that blindness has gone. We can see where before our eyes were firmly shut by illusion. Henceforth there is that in us that fixes its gaze steadfastly upon the Timeless, the Real, and the Impersonal. Insight alone has the power to pronounce on the universal truth and eternal reality of existence, because it alone has the power to penetrate the world appearance and to contemplate that bliss behind it. To this unveiled faculty, reality will then be self-evident in the same sense that we need no outside testimony or rational proof of the sun's existence: it is perfectly self-evident in our own experience.

Illumination starts as an advancing process but ends as a sudden event. We grow slowly into Overself-discovery but the glorious bloom is abrupt. Insight arises of itself and without further striving when the needful preliminaries are finished. What then happens is that there is something like a veritable turning around at the base of the whole consciousness. We realize our own immediate oneness with the ultimate by a final flash of enlightenment that effectively removes all doubts and all ignorance forever. This very first glimpse will be such a tremendous and scintillating revelation that it will leave an ineradicable impression on our minds and we can never forget what we thus learn even if we were to try. Our faith in the existence of the inner reality is thereafter absolutely unshakeable and our resolve to carry on with the quest is thereafter completely ineradicable.

Anyone who has had such a flash of insight, experience of reality, or gleam of enlightenment will naturally desire its constant presence, or at least its continued return at will. But we will find that although insight deals with what is single, ultimate, and final, there are separate graduated stages in its full unfoldment within us. The time it takes a rose to produce its buds is disproportionately longer than the time it takes these green cases themselves to open and burst into blossom. The unfoldment of insight is like that. The aspirant toils for long wearisome months or years amid emotional moods of darkness and failure, disheartenment and monotony. Suddenly the light breaks, our blindness vanishes, and we begin to see again. The flashes of enlightenment swiftly pass, but the adjustment to it of our character and mentality, life and personality spreads out over a disproportionately long period indeed. Years may often pass while we wait for the divine visitation to repeat itself. The full dawning of insight is a progressive graded event with time-lapses between each grade.

This is better understood by pursuing an analogy by which insight is usually pictured in this teaching. No more time is needed for the first glimpse of reality than is needed for a flash of lightning to streak across the sky. Hence the first dawning of insight is called in this teaching "the lightning flash." Plato has similarly described this particular characteristic of the arising of insight in his Seventh Epistle. He writes, "It is brought to birth in the soul on a sudden, as light that is kindled by a leaping spark." Indeed, the glimpse is so swift and hence so elusive that its recipient must be smart and alert to seize its dazzling significance before it is gone. It will not stay but vanishes in less than a second. Hence Augustine gives this advice: "In this first flash when thou art as if struck by lightning, when thou hearest inwardly the affirmation 'Truth,' there remain if thou canst." The intellect must handle this mystical "flash" as delicately as though it were a fragile orchid. Over-analysis may lead to its destruction, under-analysis to its incomprehension.

The student first sees reality as a person sitting in a dark room sees some of the objects therein when they are suddenly lit up by lightning, which is too swift to do more than outline the interior somewhat dimly. This degree of insight may be likened to seeing the figure of a human being from a distance but not being able to recognize whether it is a man or a woman. Hence if we miss, as we probably will, much of this significance on the first occasion, this should warn us to be better prepared when it comes again. Every further flash makes the different things more and more distinguishable from one another. Just as during the first flash of lightning observers may see only the inside walls of a room, during the second flash they may also see a table and some chairs, during the third flash they may also see some persons who are present too, until they finally get to understand what the room is really like, so the student discovers that each momentary flash of the philosophic insight as and when it occurs tends to round out and complete the visible picture.

Nevertheless the fact remains that these glimpses of reality are but momentary ones, however many times they are repeated. When each lightning flash has passed, the student has to live on and by its unforgettable remembrance in the form of a powerful intuition but not a steady perception. Thus the need arises of progression into the second stage when it is as though the same person who formerly saw a room lit up by single and fitful lightning flashes now sees the same room lit up by a small oil lantern. The light is now steady and continuous for a few hours until the oil gives out. The first brilliant lightning flash turns out to be but a foretaste of a stable state that will one day be kept as a permanent possession. Insight is brief at first, but it becomes more and more stretched out with further experience.

The third stage is when we see reality as a person in a dark room sees the objects by the light of the full moon. The fourth and the last stage is when reality is seen as objects are seen by the full light of the sun at midday.

This insight must be gained while we are still in this world in whose depths the imageless intangible Real forever abides, and not only while we are out of it in a trance. For what we see as the world is not its real nature but only a thought-construction. The waking world is partly constructed by the individual, and the individual also is partly a constructed entity. The same mind that co-constructs the one lays it before the other as an external but imagined thing. The world that is actually given in our experience is made up of millions of individual and independent items. The world that is rationally found by metaphysical examination is made of one stuff—Mind. The One appears as the Many! Thus the seeming variety of things melts down in the end to unity. All the myriad ideas not only exist for and to the mind but are in essence nothing else than Mind. Every land, mountain, and river, every wrought object, every living creature, even every human being is but a thought structure whose form appears and vanishes like the waves on an infinite ocean. The waves may subside but the ocean remains. And the ideas may go but Mind remains. It is nothing more and nothing less than the first origin and final source of all thoughts, beings, and things.

The world's objectivity and materiality exist for the individual, but for the Mind underlying both they are known as mere appearances. When, however, the individual comes to comprehend this, turns attention to this hidden Mind, and finally knows it for what it is—both when tranquilly abiding in itself or manifested in external activity—he or she is said to have attained supreme insight. All other kinds of experience deal with something as if it were apart from Mind. This alone deals with something purely pertaining to Mind itself. All other experiences deal with forms but this deals with the unique formless. The moment the mind realizes that it is itself the permanent reality behind transient appearance, the constant perceiver of its own changing thought-forms, in that moment the truth flashes across it and illusion is dispelled. For human insight is Mind contemplating itself.

Does the teaching of mentalism make the manifold world only a mirage? No! Like the superficial study of this teaching, a superficial practice of yoga seems to rob the world of reality; but an advanced practice restores it. The world finds its reality in World Mind; therefore the world is a dependent reality. Mentalism brings recognition of the physical world as being real in its own way, although only dependently real. Insight is realization of unity or spirit-matter. "There is but one Nirvana, as there is but one Truth, not two or three," Gautama Buddha told one whose mind was uncertain. The mystic has yet to see that Mind upholds all thoughts, to feel that it is present in and as all his or her external experience. People look upon this world as being either a reality or an illusion, according to whether their standpoint is materialistic or spiritualistic. The philosophic insight, however, knows that Matter is Spirit and Spirit is Matter, because it knows that both are but Mind. Therefore this opposition becomes unintelligible and does not arise.

The Overself, when not under the limitations of being aware of dreaming or unconscious, is in the fourth state; it is then its own pure Self, conscious in its own secondless way for itself, of itself, and of nothing else! The discovery of Mind in its naked pure aloneness is made in a self-absorbed psychological free state, in the thought-free, sense-free Void. But it is not enough to touch the Void, although most mystics consider it to be sufficient. The Void must next be brought into the Full; the Light must descend into the Dark; the personality must not revel in the Void for its own ecstatic enjoyment, but must convert bliss into service. This consciousness of the Void must be carried not only into every wakeful instant but also into every dreaming one. The separation into reality and appearance, into being and becoming, must now be recognized for what it is—a tentative and not a final step. Students who can rise so high must now transcend even this distinction. We must see all things as not different from the original Mind Essence, must embrace them in a single realization with the essence itself. We attain the final stage of insight only after we have passed through this earlier experience of the Void. Only then may we return to the world of appearance and penetrate its profoundest secret. And this is to perceive its oneness with the Void, its not being different from the unseen and unseeable Infinite Space. After insight into the meaning of the Void, the Naught, flashes upon us, we travel onward to gain an understanding of the All, of the universal manifestation itself. When these two stages have been mastered, when insight attains its fullest bloom, the influx of separate thoughts will no longer break our transcendental consciousness and may therefore be accepted as a part of the Real. This, the highest grade of insight, is not something that happens now and then but something that indescribably is forever present, whether during sleep or wakefulness.

Enlightenment is not a process that occurs as the result of a single factor. If insight has been gained by purely mystical means—which is the shorter way—it is always partial and fitful. If it has been gained by philosophic means—which includes the mystical and is therefore the longer way—it is full and permanent. The science of biology has shown that Nature takes more time to bring the superior organisms to their full growth than to bring the inferior ones to the same point. In the same way she requires a longer period to bring to maturity the higher power of the human mind than the lower ones. And insight, being the highest, subtlest, and most recondite of all such powers, can therefore come into being only long after the others have come into being. That is to say, scientific thought and metaphysical reflection, mundane emotion and mystical feeling, intellect and intuition must first proffer their contributions before insight can establish itself. Hence insight cannot be reached by intellect or emotion, intuition or will acting apart. None of these can of itself attain this goal. The whole person must advance toward it. When the faculty of reason is constantly exercised at its highest pitch, which means its most abstract and metaphysical pitch, if and when such exercise is conjoined in a certain way with the practice of mystical meditation, and when profound veneration and altruistic compassion is the atmosphere within which they move, they are one day suddenly and quite spontaneously replaced by the higher faculty of insight.

Mystics find their inner Self. They discover that personality is rooted in a deeper, wider being—the Overself. But they do not discover the significance of the not-self. They do not enter into comprehension of the All. Once a philosophic illumination has been gained, it shines steadily and enduringly. It is never clouded even for a moment. In other words, the philosopher walks in perpetual light and not in intermittent flashes of light as does the mystic. The philosophic knowledge is a well-established one, whereas the mystic knowledge is an occasional one. Philosophic truth is a constant and unclouded power of the one, whereas fleeting intuition or temporary ecstasy at best is the attainment of the other.

When a steady enlightenment beats down upon your path of life, you have gained something that is unquestionably superior to the fitful feelings of ecstasy that visit the devotee or the mystic now and then. For these feelings will not of themselves be sufficient to keep you from going astray during the intervals when you do not have them, whereas the philosophic illumination shows you clearly every inch of the ground where you are walking. The mystic gets fitful and partial glimpses of the Over-consciousness, whereas with the philosopher, like a lamp in a windless place, it burns steadily. The inner perception will finally become continuous and the insight into what both the person and the world really are will be inseparable from him or her. The philosopher's inward eye forever gazes into infinity while his or her physical eyes do not fail to see the world at the same time.

What are the inner characteristics whereby we will know that we have attained insight? The development of the different stages of insight—if achieved by the philosophic way—necessarily brings about certain changes of moral character as well as mental understanding. In the first stage there are: morally, the permanent enfeeblement of selfishness in the same way that a tree that has been struck by lightning is so enfeebled that it will not only stop growing but will also die sooner than it otherwise would have done; mentally, the permanent disappearance of wrong views about self and God and of old illusions about Matter, time, and space. In the second stage the moral result is a permanent enfeeblement of lust, anger, and hate. That is to say, although we may sometimes be disturbed by rebellious thoughts of ill-will and sensual desire, the thoughts themselves will not attain any strength or intensity and will not be able to endure for more than a very short time. We will soon be ready to forgive critics, for example, or to be friendly with enemies. Our partial apprehensions will be enlarged, our illusory beliefs will be eliminated, and our long habits of wrong thinking will be corrected.

In the third stage all passions are utterly subdued; lust, anger, and hate are completely effaced and can never again affect our feelings for even a moment. In the fourth stage there is a perfect balance between the just needs of egoism and the wise demands of altruism. Disinterestedness marks all dealings with other persons; vanity is utterly extinguished. There is a continuous unbroken feeling of exalted serenity that exists quite independently of the senses. All the finest tendencies of character that circumstances may have hitherto kept latent or only half-unfolded are now able to manifest themselves in their fullness without hindrance. Although the earlier stages of insight's development enable a student to intuit reality in ascending degrees of clearness, the experience is a fitful one and is necessarily followed by a recoil back into ordinary consciousness. The attainment of the fourth stage alone yields a permanent and unbroken realization throughout the lifetime. The mind is now always poised and calm and ever-concentrated on the Real. It possesses the power to enter at any moment into itself and remain rapt and thought-free. Our consciousness of the Real will be an unwavering one. Our perception of the transiency and insufficiency of form will be equally unwavering. Our satisfaction with experience of the Divine will make us feel complete.

Nevertheless the Absolute still remains a grand Mystery—even when we have won our way through to its presence and stand in its light. No human being ever becomes the Godhead. The highest possible achievement is to stand in the light of the Godhead. Thereby the whole universe becomes revealed as itself a divine thought. This is insight.

Insight is something that cannot be communicated but must be personally realized. It is entirely experiential. The guru who claims that his mere wish for others' attainment can enduringly realize itself in them, is deceiving them. It is a sure sign of such misleading doctrine when a guru declares that the path to realization leads to and through him or her alone. Just as no amount of instruction will show someone how to dream—for it must come naturally or not at all—so no amount of instruction will show someone the ultimate state. The experience must come spontaneously of itself. To expect spiritual attainment without having deserved it by one's own exertions is as unreasonable as to expect engineering attainment without having worked with an engine. The personal favor of no master and no priest can grant it, whatever popular superstition of self-interested "guides" may say to the contrary. People who think that—by wholly handing their lives over to such a guru—realization will come of itself one day without any or even a little effort on their own part, are going to receive a severe awakening. One great human delusion is that which fosters the desire to get something for nothing. The rich social parasite who is satisfied to contribute nothing but takes much from the common store merely because some family ancestor had once given something is one example; the religious devotees who expect, without any effort on their part, some other person to give them God, are another. There are too many seekers in mystical circles who are waiting for a master to appear on the horizon who will conveniently present them with what can only come as a result of their own endeavors.

Genuine teachers seek to help their pupils unfold what is already within them; they do not pretend to perform a miracle. If any teachers could permanently lift others into the Overself, if they could transfer their own consciousness of it to a second person, the feat would have been accomplished by all the great sages of the past; the history of humankind then would have been quite different and the present state of humankind far superior. It has never been done because it can never be a gift. Only through the processes of biological evolution does a sperm grow into an adult human being, and only through the processes of spiritual evolution does a person grow into a sage. There are no swift and sudden transformations. The transforming touch of grace will come at the right psychological moment of our history when it should come. But that moment is determined by our Overself, not by any other person—no matter how lauded they are as a teacher or saint.

However useful and helpful they admittedly are in their own place, teachers cannot bring anyone to the one thing that matters most—to the established realization of the Overself. That can be done only by God's grace and in God's time—not ours or theirs. No embodied intermediary can do it for anyone else, can bestow the one initiation that counts above all others, because it yields a permanent conscious and unbroken communion. In the end, instruction must come pure and undefiled by human limitations. No finite being can initiate us enduringly into the Infinite, only the Infinite itself can do that. Truth is best studied at its source. The aspirant should indeed no longer desecrate the universality of the Overself by transposing its greatness and grandeur to earthly mortals, nor sully its pure spiritual nature by anthropomorphic worship. Guru-less, we must stand alone before God. For God's deputy, the Overself, is a real being whose presence can be felt, whose understanding and consciousness do exist, and who possesses the power to respond. Hence our call will be heard, our prayer for help will not be uttered in vain if it is uttered sincerely.

While spirituality cannot be carried from one person to another as we carry a suitcase, those who are sensitive may feel its presence and power. It is quite possible for an attained master to give devoted disciples a temporary glimpse of reality by imparting to them a momentary glimpse of the first stage of insight. This he or she does by telepathically quietening disciples' thought processes and by deepening their emotional movement.

The philosophic goal cannot be achieved by mass production methods, although the religious goal may. Individuals must find their own peculiar path to it. They may find it with the help of another, of a teacher, but still it will and must be their own.

ELEVEN

Is the World an Illusion?

IT IS NOT SURPRISING that when mystics in East and West come to regard as their loftiest wisdom a metaphysic, which is statically perched on an altitude of the most abstractly conceived ideas, which is void of human relations and human interest, and which disdains the entire world as being non-existent, they also come to be regarded by the critics of mysticism as impractical dreamers. The consequences of such a degeneration are serious. People with brains put them to no better use than wasting whole lifetimes in interminable discussions of a purely logical character, discussions that are devoid on the one hand of human coloring and divorced on the other from human needs.

But we ought first to inquire whether this really is the loftiest ancient wisdom or whether it is merely the degeneration of it.

The doctrine of world illusion is a stumbling block to most Western students, and this is understandable. Many Indians themselves expound this remarkable doctrine in a manner so airy and speech so glib that one feels intuitively that to them it is only a bit of verbiage. A courageous and penetrating few have grasped the true thought of their masters; the rest repeat words and sentences like so many parrots. When we inquire as to what is the highest wisdom attained by Eastern sages, we are informed by many metaphysicians and several mystics that it consists in regarding a mysterious entity, Spirit, as the only reality and the universe itself as a mere illusion. When we ask them how this illusion originated, they reply that because this entity alone exists there are no individuals in existence and consequently nobody to be caught in illusion! When, further, we ask them what is the purpose of human existence, they answer that it is to discover reality; yet in the same breath they say that reality is totally unrelated to the universe and consequently to such existence! Nor is the current Western religious belief that this world is principally a material one with a kind of incidental spiritual "ghost" somewhere inside it any better. It is only one step less materialistic than the atheistic belief that there is no other world at all.

A doctrine that says that the Perfect alone exists, that the Absolute alone is real, that the universe is illusory, and that our knowledge of it is false—such a doctrine unconsciously and unsatisfactorily commits itself to the conclusion that the Godhead is eternally engaged in the act of self-deception! This doctrine that makes the world nonexistent, although drawn from the undeniable fact that the testimony of the senses is sometimes refuted by the testimony of reason, is a false conclusion reached by confused rational thinking or obscure mystical feeling. Nevertheless, the idea-intoxicated metaphysicians or self-deceived mystics who dismiss the universe as an ungrounded illusion do not dismiss themselves thereby. They too are a part of this illusion. Yet they continue to treat themselves as a reality. Such inconsistency alone would show the futility of their efforts and the illogicality of their thinking.

The orthodox doctrine of an immobilized, inactive Reality can never explain why the universe is present in experience nor why we feel we are here at all. But we need not accept this doctrine as being the best that mysticism has to offer. Quite correctly this metaphysic proclaimed that humans attained the higher goal when they came to recognize their true being as rooted in or identical with the Absolute being. Quite incorrectly, however, through losing itself in queer and questionable logical abstractions, it converted the individual self into a pale fiction and the physical world into a grotesque hallucination. The truth is that neither is the one a fiction nor the other a hallucination, but both are a manifestation. However insufficiently, the Real reveals itself in them. It cannot be sundered from them.

Those among the Greek, the Alexandrian, and the Indian mystical metaphysicians who opposed the reality of Spirit to the illusion of Matter, were unable to explain how the two could be unified. Consequently, they placed the former on a pinnacle separated by an unbridgable chasm from the creative Universal Soul, from the material world, and from the individual soul. All their ingenious explanations of existence either stopped at the edge of this chasm and there left the Absolute as an inexplicable mystery with whom the Relative had nothing to do, or left the manifested world as a purposeless creation drifting like a mist in mid-air. Only one bridge can be built across this chasm and only mentalism can build it.

We have seen that "matter" is non-existent and we know that thoughts are transient. What is it then that we are dealing with as the stuff of our personal world experience? Mentalism answers that it is the permanent essence of all thoughts, that it is Mind. This discovery is as far as we can get when searching inward. Mind Essence is the irreducible ultimate reality. It is itself empty of all forms, void of all individualization. But we have also to search outward. And then, when we are able to see that it does not make any *intrinsic* difference to itself whether it be known as transient thoughts or as enduring Thought, so long as it is *always* perceived as present, we see aright. The world is an appearance if it be viewed as a process, but it is the uniquely Real if viewed as a single substance.

When first the truth dawns on us that this mysterious all-enclosing yet paradoxically all-excluding Void is the Real; when, second, its blessed presence is felt as something living within us in all states and times and places and not merely in meditation alone; when, third, we see the universe in its Cause and its Cause in the universe—Matter in Spirit and Spirit in Matter, the two at once—we are said to possess insight. We then perceive that the broad brown earth, covered with green stuff and rolling through hills and valleys, is not less real in substance than the Void, not less divine in essence even though its form be but a mental image that must pass away. We feel that it is a part of the mysterious Whole, a part that can in no wise be separated from that which sustains and cherishes it. Thus we learn not only that there is no reality independent of Mind and no ultimate being apart from our own innermost egoless Self, but also that there exists no formed thing in our external experience that does not get its essential being from the same source whence we derive our own.

The impenetrable and enigmatic problem of how the Absolute became the Relative is a manufactured one. It exists only in a wordy realm of a logic divorced from fact, of a metaphysic that has set up an artificial opposition between Spirit and Matter because it did not know that these were merely Mind and its Idea. For if we intellectually throw everything into Mind, we discover at once the unifying principle that can neatly contain them without doing violence to its own integrity. Mind thus becomes the first principle of all existence and, paradoxically, also the last. The ego and the ego's world are ideas of the Overself and the Overself in its turn is a ray of the Mind. Just as the sun appears to have split itself up into millions of rays but nevertheless remains the same single sun that it was before, so the ineffable Mind cannot be separated into parts except in appearance, and cannot be divided into individual entities except in human thinking of it. Those who believe that Mind has ever lost anything by this self-giving, has ever become less than it ever was, do not comprehend it. It always keeps its pristine, undivided, and integral character. We humans are in essence Divine Souls radiated from that central sun—a simile that is useful to help our thinking minds grasp, in the only way they can, both the intimacy and immediacy of our inner reality. We are sharers in the reflection of its glorious light.

The One does not *become* the Many, for the orders of being and consciousness are different. It remains what it is and from it *emanates* the Many. The universe is much more an emanation than a manifestation. Because it is an emanation rather than an illusion, the World Idea is not to be treated as a non-entity. It is not to be sharply divided from reality. For it *is* the Real manifesting something of itself in a particular way. All events are only its activity as all things are only its attributes. Relativity exists between the ideas themselves but the substratum out of which they spring is the eternal and infinite, the self-existent and Absolute Mind. Matter thus becomes but a mental entity. The Absolute is not cleft inseparably from the Relative for the Relative is its own Idea. Mind itself is that which has always existed, which is the unique essence of all things and all beings, the first and last Principle of the world process. We may say of it what we may say of nothing else except Infinite Space: It *is*. And this will still be true even if the whole universe, including the conscious beings in it, disappears. Mind could not have come into existence at any specific time as it could not have come into existence from nothing; therefore, it must always have existed and there was never a moment when it was not.

By contrast, both our thoughts and the world that is inseparably associated with them are transient and changeful. But the Mind that makes their appearance possible is not. It alone can stand the supreme test of Ultimate Reality, the test of whether it is changeless and ever-enduring. Whatever is real can never perish. Whatever is only an emanation from the Real will lose its form but nevertheless will not lose its essence. If it is true that the Godhead transcends all finite things, nevertheless it is inseparably immanent in them and is indeed the very foundation of their existence. As if this cosmos could lie outside the force whence it arose, or the force outside the cosmos! They are not really two things but two aspects of one thing. It is not that the world is non-existent; it is a thought and has mental existence. Our natural desire to be assured of our own and the world's existence, no less than of life's utility, is satisfied by the truth. Thus the world problem that eluded these metaphysicians and mystics is smoothly elucidated by mentalism. But to achieve this success we must first clearly understand that mentalism is not merely the same as idealism but is a fuller doctrine. Whereas the latter would convert everything into separate ideas and leave the world as such, the former would convert them into ideas only to unify them again into this single stuff—Mind.

The Real and its appearance are the same thing seen from different sides. After all, the innumerable subjects in the latter are formed by a process of thought, which is a power belonging to the former. We cannot do violence to the world's existence by dismissing it as unreal. It is only an incomplete mysticism or an unillumined and merely intellectual metaphysics and not insight-based philosophy that attempts to do so. Philosophy, by dissolving the world's plurality into unity, reveals that it is ultimately made of the same stuff as its eternal ground. All the different space-time levels of the universe are interpenetrated by Mind. Therefore, all worlds are one. Those who live in one particular space-time level will naturally have a different form of consciousness from those who live in another one. Consequently there can be—and are—numerous forms of consciousness, each one representing a world to its inhabitants. But the ultimate "stuff" of these worlds is one and the same—Mind—only the modes of apprehending it change from one space-time level to another. Each world is real in the experience of those in it, although vastly different from the others.

No world is an illusion, for every world is spun out of God's own being; but our particular space-time mode of experiencing and knowing that world is illusory. The world appearance is real enough to those who have to live in it. Therefore the true position is not between it as illusion and something transcendental as reality, but between appearance and its hidden ground. Thus when we expand our understanding of the physical world we discover that it too is divine. So long as the myth of multiplicity holds sway over our mind, so long will we be confounded and bewildered. We must turn to the truth: unity. There is nothing but Mind.

WISDOM FOR LIVING

When we can grasp this concept, that Mind is the only reality and that all else is but its appearance or manifestation, and when we grasp the corollary of this concept, that humans themselves are fundamentally rooted in Mind—we may then proceed to the further step that if human existence has any ultimate aim at all, it can only be to demonstrate the oneness of being and to enter consciously into its own hidden truth. Thus our final conclusion must be not that the world is an illusion, nor that it is unreal, but that its externality to Mind is illusory and its independence of our own self is unreal. It does not exist in its own right. That stable reality that we believe to be in things but believe wrongly to be in their sense-experienced existence, actually resides therefore in the Universal Mind that manifests itself in them. Consequently our total impression of the world's reality is not illusory but it is misplaced. If we would lay hold of this reality in the right way we must rise above the level of sensed perceptions and attain the level of the one all-unifying Universal Mind behind them.

This mentalist appraisal of the nature of the wakeful world of so-called illusion, and this realist appraisal of its worth, are not Western alone. Thousands of years ago some wise initiated commentators on the Mandukya Upanishad, including the most ancient of all, Gaudapada, followed the same line. The teaching of the old Eastern masters was that the world does not exist except through the Self. Therefore they called the whole created universe *maya*—a word that we translate badly as "illusion" but whose true meaning can be reached only by pondering over mentalism. They pointed out that our first and natural instinct is to accept the external world as the final reality, but since that world requires a conscious self to witness it and to receive the reports of the sense organs concerning its existence, the ultimate reality was then this conscious witnessing Self. This declaration did not destroy the first acceptance of external reality; it simply supplemented and deepened it. The mentalist doctrine of maya explains that if we are not aware of the world, then the world has no real existence *for us*. Those last two words need treble underlining, for most people conveniently forget them or stupidly ignore them. Consciousness is thus shown to be the basic reality. Hence the Upanishad verse:

In me arose the whole world:
In me exists the All
In me it passes.

The false opposition of Spirit and Matter, the disheartening tenet that the material universe is without significance, and the pitiful belief that all existence is mere illusion represent the lamentable result of the impact of the full truth upon half-prepared minds.

If these views were ever to be carried into practical life, they would smite their holders with complete paralysis. The intellect would cease to move, the heart to feel, and the body to act. But whatever may have been the case in ancient or medieval times, if we look into the practical life of their present-day advocates, we find that all this talk of a futile Absolute, eternally divorced from a meaningless universe, is mere syllogistic jugglery and logical gymnastics; for they usually take as much interest in securing "illusory" earthly benefits for themselves as do the much-despised realists. While they insist for the benefit of other persons on the nothingness of the common world, actually they show no less insistence than others on treating it in terms of the utmost reality. This is an evidence of the uselessness of a metaphysic divorced from mystical science and of the danger of exaggerating a single aspect of existence at the cost of all the others. In any case, it is clear enough that the only reasonable goal of one who sincerely follows the consequences of all such teaching is to renounce the active world and become a carefree lotus-eater, a body-hating monk, or a self-centered dreamer.

Such a complete splitting of life from wisdom, of truth from experience, as is represented by the basic doctrine of this so-called highest wisdom is not likely to be acceptable to the West as a contribution from the East. Fortunately, this teaching is not worthy of the title. In the East's own hidden teaching lies a superior doctrine that satisfies alike the demands of reason, the dictates of the heart, the promptings of intuition, and the needs of practical activity. While it rigorously refuses to accept the finality and errors of sense-experience, it does not pessimistically alienate us from the ultimate values of such experience. There is no rest, no peace, no truth, no life even, certainly no happiness, while we cling to the phenomenal passing show *for its own sake;* but there is final peace and complete fulfillment when we can accept it as a fleeting manifestation of the deathless Real. Then we can convert all things and all creatures into thoughts; the myriad of thoughts into their single element, mind; and mind into its unmanifest, un-individuated infinite essence or reality, Mind. We arise to a region where all exists within ourselves and nothing can therefore be lost, where death is a fiction and suffering a phase that will pass. This is God, Nirvana, Overself—any name we wish to give it, although no name can ever reach it. It is not to be thought of as a second thing apart from ourselves, but as our very being. We are here on earth to find that.

This quest cannot be finished merely by an intellectualist abstraction of what are thought to be the illusions of the terrestrial sphere, and certainly not by ascetic flight from them. It can come to a final terminus only when insight into the Real is gained from and amid the fullest activity in the terrestrial sphere itself.

If we want to think truly of the supreme reality, we must think of it under two aspects: the ever-resting and the ever-working, and under two forms: stillness and motion. Nor can we stop our understanding of this great truth at this point. For if we want to live more truly in accordance with the way in which the life of God itself is lived, if we aspire to imitate the divine existence so far and so humbly as we dare, then we too must bring our little lives into this same two-fold rhythm of quiescent stillness and busy activity, of inward contemplation and outward struggle, of self-regarding satisfaction and altruistic service.

This remembrance of and concentration on the silent Void while engaged in the midst of bustling activity is admittedly not easy and requires nothing less than genius for its successful consummation. It is called in the Chinese hidden teaching "Wu Wei." An adulterated fragment of this teaching exists in Lao Tzu's little text entitled Tao Te Ching and the phrase is usefully translated as meaning "non-doing" or "inaction." Both Western and Eastern mystics have erroneously thought this means to refrain from action by living in monastic retreat. The correct meaning is the inner realization of the basic voidness, the immateriality of existence, while outwardly taking that materiality as real for practical purposes. To practice inaction, in the sense in which it has been used in Eastern mystical works like the Bhagavad Gita and the Tao Te Ching, does not mean physical inertia. This is a materialistic misapprehension. It means to effect an entrance into the Void *and then* to carry the sense of its emptiness into the very midst of activity, into the heart of physical existence. We have to comprehend that, despite appearances, the hidden teaching does not lead to utter nihilism or to blank negativism, but rather to what is most real in life. Hence if most mystics envisage their ultimate physical goal as a state of inspired inactivity, all philosophers envisage their ultimate physical goal as a state of inspired action.

If it be true that we all live and move and have our being in the Infinite Mind, it must be equally true that the presence of that Mind is not confined to any ashram, mountain cave, or cloistered retreat. It is here in London, here in Chicago, and here in Chungking, too. It is just as much here in the midst of Broadway's bustle and London's teeming life as it is in any far-off Tibetan monastery. If we could not find it while attending to our everyday practical interests, if it were utterly outside and forever beyond them, then it would not be the Real. If the start of outward activity annuls the inward peace, then the true transcendence has not been found. When we understand that this world is a manifestation of divine reality itself, then this earthly life is emphatically not a trap set by Satan as some believe, nor a mirage made of cloud as others say. It is not only something that does matter but, on the contrary, something that must matter even more to the truth-finder than it does to the materialist.

TWELVE

Ascetic Mysticism Reconsidered

WE OFTEN HEAR that all religious and mystical paths lead to the same goal—God. This is doubtless true if we take a long-range evolutionary view of existence, if we think in terms of hundreds of lifetimes rather than a single one. But if we descend from ultimate to immediate considerations, we shall find that there are important differences among the attainments of the different paths. Mysticism is a strange country. It is no less important to find out the hidden goal or intrinsic purpose of a mystical technique than it is to understand the person who has originated it. For in this elusive terrain, it is easy to jump to a superficial estimate but hard to descend to a scientific one. It is not enough to accept the asserted objective of any such path. Its examination is equally necessary. "Does it really lead to such an objective?" is the question that must start this examination, and not only by the declared theories behind it, but much more by its ascertained results, are we to find a correct answer. It is thus that my own new pilgrimage was born.

It all began with the framing of a single and simple question that experience, reflection, and other people had suggested to me. I wanted to know why mystics play such an insignificant part in the collective life of humankind when, if their theories are true and their powers exist, they ought to be playing a leading part. For I believed then, and even more so now, that the ultimate worth of an outlook on life that inculcates the hidden unity of the human family is its power to find expression in the earthly life of humankind. I believe that those who possess such an outlook should endeavor to render it effectual, first in their own everyday existence, and second in that of society, and not be content only with dreaming or talking about it. I believe that there is laid upon them the duty to *try* to mold, however slightly, the public mind; to *try* to guide the contemporary public welfare movements and to inspire; to *try* to influence or counsel the leaders and intelligentsia. They should not find an excuse for their failure to do so in the public distaste for mysticism, for they are not asked to obtrude the subject itself, but only its fruits in useful service and wise guidance. Nor ought they to refuse the task as foredoomed to failure in the face of evil public karma. It is their duty to try, unconcernedly, leaving all results to the Overself. In short, if their claims to esoteric knowledge and extraordinary powers are worth anything at all and can be demonstrated by results, they ought to try to leave their mark on history in a most unmistakable manner.

But when we gaze around at the contemporary world, we actually behold no such effective contribution, even though we are living in an epoch that has witnessed the most dramatic convulsions of human history. Whatever social benefit has been brought by the mystics to humankind has mostly been brought not because of their mystical outlook but in spite of it.

Mystical hermits who withdraw from their fellows physically may in time withdraw their fellow-feeling from them, too. When they settle down to enjoy the inward peace that world-shunning will admittedly yield, there arises the danger of a complete introversion of the sympathies, a callous self-centeredness in social relations and a cold indifference to the fate of humankind. We see it in the persons of ascetics and yogis especially, who—because they are so sublimely wrapped up in their own inner peace—are regarded as perfect sages by an ignorant populace and are honored accordingly. We must not fail to note the implication that the millions of suffering human creatures would then share in this supposed non-existence. Such a crankily ascetic and confusedly metaphysical indifference to the world leads inevitably to an indifference toward all humankind. Its welfare is not their concern. Thus, from a social standpoint they become impotent. To show, in the face of world agony, an emotional callousness and an intellectual apathy is a spiritual greatness that I have no desire to attain. On the contrary, I would regard it as spiritual littleness.

Such reflections alone might have sufficed to persuade me to take up the pilgrim's staff again, but is a further defect of the mystical temperament (a defect that, of course, I shared although fortunately my mental make-up was too rational and too complex not to be somewhat aware of it) that it is prone to find plausible esoteric excuses for the inexcusable. The destiny that has led me thus far had to step in, therefore, and bring me to the critical crossroads of a compulsory and decisive recognition of the need for further search for a higher source of truth. And I began to do this, firstly through a painful personal experience of monastic institutions that had quickly descended the way of most "spiritual" institutions, and secondly, by stripping away the facade of glamor that surrounded those whom I had taken at their reputed status of perfect sages when they were only perfect yogis at best. The consequence of this was a reorientation, or rather return, toward my early love of philosophy in an effort to correct and balance my mystical experience.

MYSTICISM AND POLITICS

Before I can explain this observation, I must first pen a brief pre-amble. There is a common belief that writers on a higher thought should avoid politics, but it is a belief common only among the mystically inclined or monastically minded, not among the philosophically trained. I shall shortly explain that the only kind of mysticism I follow is the philosophical kind. Now it is, among several other things, part of the business of philosophy to examine political principles and ethical problems. It might, however, be advisable for mystics, religionists, and ascetics to avoid political discussions, at least from the standpoint of practical policy, or they will run the risk of starting schisms and opening splits in their ranks and institutions because they distribute their political allegiance in various quarters. But such a risk does not detain the philosophically inclined for a moment. The latter are necessarily independent and subserve the interests of no racial group, no particular organization, and no special political affiliation. They believe truth to be as necessary in this practical world as in the less-visited worlds of metaphysical doctrine. Truth is their primary business, but it is ample enough to include matters erroneously supposed to be remote from it.

Nevertheless, those accustomed to move in the fixed orbit of ascetic mysticism, with its aloofness from politics as an expression of its aloofness from all earthly things, may be surprised or even shocked at the thought that a professed mystic should put forth such ideas as will be found in the next few pages. Many may consequently misjudge them and think that I am stooping into the dust of politics or airing nationalistic prejudices. Those friends, however, who really know me will not make this error. For I have come too often on this planetary scene and thus lived too long to care for the politics of a moment when eternity is my native atmosphere. I have traveled too widely and reflected too deeply to take root overmuch in any one land rather than another and can honestly say with Thomas Paine, "The world is my country!" I have found loyal, loving friends and bitter malicious enemies in every continent, among the Asians as among the Westerners, among capitalists no less than communists, and have come to regard all peoples with a more or less equal and cosmopolitan eye, knowing that it is always and ever the individual *character* that counts.

If a person has genuinely awakened into the Overself-consciousness, the experience will of itself annihilate prejudices and unite him or her fundamentally with others. If anyone speaks of God but dislikes another merely because of racial or color difference, be sure he or she is still living in darkness. Materialists who think they are the body and nothing else, naturally betray racial prejudice. Mentalists who know that they are mind more than flesh, naturally discard such prejudice as puerile. My views are therefore quite detached and impartial. If I venture now into what seems like politics for a few minutes, it is only because I do not and cannot divorce anything—not even politics—from life and hence from truth and reality. I have no use for a goodness that wastes itself like a lonely flower in the desert air, nor for self-admiring monastic retreats, as I have no use for a faith or doctrine that is to be confined to the inactive shelves of libraries or the fitful gossip of tea tables.

I cannot fail to admit some justice in a further question, another that is often asked me by Western critics: why has Shangri-la, which is the traditional home of yoga and the reputed paradise of mystics, shown proportionately such little external benefit from their presence and powers? Such a question may irritate many Shangrians emotionally, but it always impresses itself intellectually on most Westerners.

Tibet, even more than any other part of Asia, has fallen victim to the seductions of ascetic and monastic mysticism. The grand spiritual goal is there thought to demand complete isolation for its attainment. The most advanced spiritual type is believed to be the complete recluse. What has been the practical social result of all this lofty aspiration? Dirt, semi-starvation, disease, and superstition are the common heritage of the masses, for those who had the superior intelligence to instruct and help them did not care to do so, did not care to take an interest in such mundane matters. To varnish the picture of the "Forbidden Land" with the romantic glamor of mystery is to deceive oneself. [Editor's note: In a conversation in 1981, Dr. Brunton expressed pleasure that the present Dalai Lama had not only recognized these problems but also had been successful in his efforts to reintroduce a more philosophical perspective to Tibetan Buddhist thought and practice.]

I came for the first time as a world-indifferent mystic, seeking to penetrate into the mystery of Shangri-la. I left for the last time as a world-observant philosopher, having penetrated into the misery of Shangri-la. Why have the yogis and lamas been so ineffectual in modern Asia, as the mystics have been so powerless in modern Europe? The idealism that places defective observation on the pedestal of virtue, which is unable to see what is happening all around it and which ignores all the realities of a situation when they do not fit in with its wishful thinking, is not the kind in which my search for truth could continually afford to indulge.

I foresee that quite a number of people, bewildered by what the West has spiritually *been* in the past and dazzled by what the East has spiritually *taught* in the past, will fall prey to an increasing flow of swamis and monks, gurus and yogis, who will either invade the West or else invite would-be followers to leave it altogether and enter their ashrams. And even those who fail to fall for the Eastern varieties may fall for their corresponding Western analogues; freak forms of mysticism and occultism are emerging for their benefit out of fertile Euro-American imaginations. Already some Shangrian gurus have appointed advance agents (who are Westerners themselves) in Western lands to collect followers, gather disciples, give "initiations," or persuade aspirants to join their organizations. They are working without the benefit of publicity's limelight, partly in order to foster the inspiring illusion of representing a secret fraternity. And they are working with great success. It is enough for them to gain a single follower and then ask him to start the missionary snowball rolling. He or she at once informs his friends, who inform others and so on, ad infinitum. It is such a rare and thrilling opportunity, they tell themselves: "Just fancy! To become the disciple of a real master while staying at home in America or England, without having to travel on a long journey to Shangri-la and live there for years. It is all so easy, too." Hence they tumble over each other in their haste to join—and needless to say, everyone is accepted.

Those contemporaries—and they are few indeed—who fled from the turmoil of life and have found satisfaction and peace in secluded Indian ashrams or their Western equivalents, do not represent modern humankind but are rather atavistic throwbacks to more primitive times and more obsolete outlooks, persons quite understandably repelled by the complexity and strain of present-day life. Unfortunately, they overlook the fact that it is precisely to understand such complexity and to master such struggle that the God they profess to obey has thrown them into modern Western bodies. Do they seriously believe that they are reborn on earth only to pass through the same experience and the same environment each time? No! Life is perennially fresh and they return to learn new lessons from new experiences in new surroundings. To shrink from the difficult present and retreat to the easier past, to evade the problems of modernity by taking refuge in antiquity, to gain no inspiration from their own resources and to lapse back into those of medieval people, is to become defeatists. But it would be utterly wrong for me to hinder such persons from making good their escape. Let them do so by all means, if they wish. Nothing here written is intended for them.

The war was their chance to wake up, to quicken their process of thought. If it did not open the eyes of these mystical Rip Van Winkles, then its bestial horror and fiery terror was for them in vain. If the war did not break their unhealthy bewitchment, then the postwar period certainly cannot do so. Mystics who remained mere spectators of the world conflict may have kept their inner peace undisturbed. But there is no need to practice yoga to obtain this kind of negative peace. Every inhabitant of a graveyard has it. I write only for the others and they are the majority—who are sufficiently aroused not to fall into an escapism that merely evades the problems of living and does not solve them, who do not wish to revert to spiritual atavism in a progressive world, who have been stirred by humankind's wartime agonies to seek the rugged road to truth no less than the smoother path to peace, and who have come to understand that the only satisfactory question is the one that combines the pursuit of both truth and peace with the unselfish service of humanity. [PB is referring to World War II, but his references to war and world crises also apply to the current world situation.]

MYSTICISM'S RETREAT

Mysticism has been associated in the popular mind mostly with monasteries, retreats, ashrams, caves, and similar places where novices and would-be yogis foregathered. Thus it came to be looked upon as a way of escape from the domestic difficulties, business troubles, and emotional disappointments that seem so inseparable from human existence. Those who could not cope with the ups and downs of daily life, with the shocks of unexpected misfortune or the death of beloved relatives, abruptly detached themselves from society and fled to the relative peace of monastic life. Those who could not qualify themselves to earn their livelihood by burdensome physical or mental labor, renounced further effort and raised both their failure and their incompetence to the pedestal of virtue by proclaiming that they had renounced the world with all its wickedness! Nevertheless, deviously or directly, all these types came to the world for alms and food and clothing, for which the world continued to struggle, thus rendering itself able to provide them with their needs. Nor did they hesitate to proclaim a lordly spiritual superiority—quite disproportionate at times to their own personal defects—over the worldlings who financed or fed them.

If people have undergone great emotional disappointments or much worldly suffering, they have every excuse for fleeing away to the peaceful refuge of monasticism, usually symbolized in the East by the donning of a yellow robe. What cannot be excused is, first, if they rest for the remainder of their earthly existence in such "escapism"; and second, the large number of unholy "holy" people who hypocritically imitate such persons and put on yellow robes, cover their heads with ashes, or appoint themselves to manage ashrams in order to beg, covertly or openly, their way through life—or worse, so as to exploit the pious or the aspirational. They contribute nothing to society and follow no inner quest for themselves, but batten on the superstitious hopes and panicky fears of the ignorant multitude by bestowing utterly worthless pseudo-blessings. Thus they unconsciously exhibit the very materialism that they are supposed to avoid! And they have their parallel types in the mystic cults and occult circles of the West, too. When mysticism becomes merely a way of escape from difficulties that sharply demand to be faced, or when it breeds an atmosphere wherein pious charlatans can pretend to be hallowed mouthpieces for God, it is time to call a critical halt.

Mental quiet alone, however perfect, is of itself not enough. People who are content with it are not complete. For life is here and now, and to live only in mystical delights in the belief that they are the ultimate goal is to live only at the dream level. The consequence is that the external everyday life of action is kept outside them; it is left untouched or even regarded with positive hostility. If we understand with the philosophers that meditation is for life, it is well; but if we can understand only with the mystics that life is for meditation, then it is not well.

There are those who believe philosophy to be a synonym for idleness. Yet its quest is a virile affair—not a resignation to lethargy, a dissolution into inertia, nor an excuse for inaction. This is a quest that does not lead into ascetic negation of the world but into philosophic mastery of such negation, not into self-centered apathy but into altruistic, wise, and useful activity. Whereas ascetic mysticism rejects the world, integral philosophy annexes it. Mysticism must become a part of life, not an evasion of it.

Every person has to act in some way; it is impossible for anyone to live without action. The ascetic, who thinks he or she has renounced it, has merely substituted one kind of action for another. This being the case, philosophy says it is better to align the *motives* for action with the highest philosophic ideal. All lesser motives are merely means to some end, whereas this alone is an end in itself. Ascetics who, as an end in itself, cut off contact with the world and shrink from its affairs, will surely drift into sterile negation; whereas the ones who regard it only as an instrumental aid to personal peace and mental self-discipline will intermittently return to the world they deserted and embrace its affairs. Thus, they may test the true worth of their attainment by adjusting it to active life, assure themselves whether the calmness that they have gained in a quiet corner can be kept in a noisy one, and help those who are unable to escape even temporarily from the world.

Now the sheltered life of an ashram may weaken a person for the struggle of existence, or it may strengthen him or her. Everything depends on the instruction, or lack of it, given in the ashram, the breadth of the external experience, and the internal status achieved by its director. In any case, such methods of mass retreat are unsuited to us of the modern world and especially the Western world. It is better at least to remain human beings, since our feet are still encased in shoe leather and we have to walk this earth. Was it not a wise German who said: "He who has experienced nothing is made no wiser by solitude?"

Dwight Goddard, translator of *A Buddhist Bible,* after having qualified himself by study in China and Japan among the monks, ascetics, hermits, and scholars, made several attempts to found an ashram, a Buddhist retreat, both in the mountains of Vermont at Thetford and on the shores of California at Santa Barbara. Later he wrote me that he had most unfortunate experiences in each case, so he decided in the end that America was not ready for such an experiment. This confirms my own view that it is not because the West is not ready for such things, but because it has outgrown them, that it has refused to flee into asceticism and escapism. Each incarnation carries its special and necessary lessons for us, however disagreeable they may be. Therefore, the attempt to shirk those lessons by falling into an escapist attitude and environment is in no way praiseworthy.

I am not undervaluing the past, however. It has a definite value. But if we are to progress, we have only to learn from it and then put it aside—not to live in it stubbornly, blindly. We must look to present needs. Modern people can find no foothold in systems that are based on antique needs and that seem so utterly remote from contemporary life; in fact, if they are wide-awake, they not only dislike them but frequently even distrust them. We must beware of such atavism, such seeking to escape by a regression from the struggle of modern conditions to the shelter of primitive ones. The goal of our fitful human existence cannot be so narrow and so negative as to idolize the life of a lotus-eater, to lull people into continual trances or half-trances, or to let them meditate themselves into a permanent condition of dreamy futility. Nor can it be to indulge all one's years in the joyous hiatus of emotional titillations. Rare, however, are those determined mystics who succeed in emancipating themselves from the fanatical extreme of excessive meditation without falling into the other error of abandoning it altogether. Great indeed is the person who can escape from the pitfall of being carried away by ecstatic feelings into an anesthesia of social action. The ascetic who sits in negative virtue and safe isolation from the world's fray may feel happy, but the sage who spurns such egoistic satisfaction and serves others in its tumultuous midst provides a better ideal. Such a life is a creative one and is not stippled with the pale hues of futility.

SERVING THE GOOD OF ALL

The question therefore arises: are mystics to continue playing the old part of being passive spectators of the world-show or are they going to measure up to this unique opportunity to render timely service? Those who have been gifted with a glimpse of the far-off divine goal, toward which all things are moving, should realize that they have a worthwhile place in the present scheme, a place that they alone can fill. They can contribute what no one else can. They can not only help, as every decent person is helping, the forces of righteousness to secure outward victory over the forces of wickedness, but they can also assist in the equally important inward struggle of the forces of knowledge against those of ignorance.

Anchorites who sit in a vacuum cut off from the world, which they cannot cope with and which they lack the imaginative sympathy to understand, have, if they are sufficiently intelligent and sufficiently developed, to face an inner crisis today. The world war and its aftermath involves us all, including them. Either they must be stirred by the tremendous happenings into a realization of their social responsibility and moral duty, or they must be written off humanity's account as contemporary failures. They must wake up to the new world situation. How can people of head and heart remain foreigners to the tragic external forces around them today?

How can those who feel with and for their suffering fellows, who recognize this unique war for the spiritual conflict that it really is, who understand the tremendous moral consequences for humankind's future involved in its outcome—how can such persons shut themselves up in the ivory towers of yogic ashrams and monastic retreats? This callous disregard of other people's miseries, this encampment in a splendid oasis kept all to oneself, this ostrich-like immurement in a cold ivory tower, is not a sign of sagehood, whatever the populace believe. It was Vasishta, an ancient sage not an ascetic, who said: "Unless the good of all becomes your good, you will add only fetters to your feet," when urging a young prince, who Buddha-like sought to renounce the world and escape its duties to gain an egocentric peace. Whoever truly understands and deeply feels an inner relationship with and a shared responsibility for fellow creatures can never subscribe to the cult of indifference. In a world crisis like the present one, for example, such ones could never sit idly by, babbling with shrugged shoulders of people having to bear their karma and of everything being just as God wishes it to be, while aggressive human instruments of unseen evil forces strive to fix spiked manacles upon the human race and mind. On the contrary, they will rise to the imperative call of the hour.

It is on this point of the necessity for altruistic service that the philosophic path diverges strikingly from the mystic path. Such a divergence, needful though it was at all times, has become more needful than ever in our own times. The day of spiritual isolation has passed. Such a self-centered doctrine can make little appeal to those who have been touched by the desperate and urgent needs of modern humankind. Mysticism seeks a static condition, whereas philosophy seeks a dynamic one. Mysticism is content with withdrawal from life, but philosophy would embrace all life. Mystics are happy when they obtain their *own* inner peace, but philosophers will be happy only when all get such peace. The serene state that mantles philosophers is not bought at the price of self-centered indifference to others and does not isolate them from their struggles. Philosophers are subject to an inner necessity to serve humankind.

The great sages saw the desperate need of humankind and compassionately gave what help they could. They never stood aloof; they did not despise those who had to participate in worldly life and flee from them accordingly, but understood their situation and helped them. They did not spend their lives sitting apart in mountain caves and forest retreats, in ashrams and monastic hideouts, but went where the crowds were, where they were needed, in fact. This is what Jesus did. This is what Buddha did. Jesus indeed worked so untiringly for the enlightenment of others that he often took no time to eat. This, indeed, is the outstanding characteristic that distinguishes them from mere yogis. They had pity; they had fellow feeling. In the Bhagavad Gita, Krishna makes it perfectly plain that the yogi who lives in and serves the world is far superior to the yogi who flees from and renounces it. Yet despite this explicit teaching by the one most-revered Indian sage, many Hindu ascetics will tell you that self-centered monasticism is superior!

Whoever has attained true and permanent insight does not need to spend his or her time always in meditation. For meditation is a form of mental exercise to help its practitioner get into the transcendent consciousness of pure Mind. One who sees pure Mind all the time does not need to practice any exercise for its possible perception. When, therefore, we are told that a sage lives in remote places and mountain caves in order to practice his or her meditations undisturbed, we may be sure that this person is only an aspirant, only a would-be sage. The populace, impressed by this asceticism and awed by his or her trance, often regard such a yogi as a sage. He or she may accept such a valuation. But this yogi will really possess the status only of a mystic, perhaps even a perfect one. If mystics reach such perfection and are bewitched by transient trances, they will feel that they are all-sufficient and do not need anything from the world. The corollary of this, unfortunately, is that the woes of others have nothing to do with them also. If they begin fascinated by the emotional satisfaction that envelops their achievement, they develop an indifference toward suffering humankind and end by becoming complacent recluses and nothing more. This does not mean that sages will never practice meditation. They will. But they will do so more for the benefit of others than for their own. They will carry out all their other personal and social responsibilities, as their wisdom and karmic circumstances dictate; sages will certainly not seek to run away from them nor believe that their enlightenment has relieved them of others.

An appreciation of all the admirable benefits of mystic practice should not blind us to its limitations and make us commit the error of setting it up as the only goal for all humankind. Reflective people will sooner or later come up against these limitations and the discontent thus generated will cause them to bestir themselves once more upon this quest of the Overself. Thus they may eventually enlarge their horizons and perceive that the ideal type is not the mystic but the sage.

What is a sage? The sage is the person who has finished all three stages of religion, yoga, and philosophy, has realized the Overself, and has come in consequence to a wide compassion for fellow creatures.

Because the sage comprehends that the root of most human troubles and sufferings is ignorance, he or she likewise comprehends that the best form of service that can be rendered is to enlighten others. Hence so far as circumstances and capacities permit, and so far as the aspiration of others indicates, sages devote themselves to their inner welfare. In such a beneficent occupation they will therefore incessantly engage themselves. Through all history the mystic has been confused with the sage simply because the latter has rarely existed, being usually an aspirational ideal rather than a realized possibility. The highest type of the former achieves what may be called "yogic immobilization," which is brought about by following a path of abstraction from entanglements, a path that is a necessary mental and physical discipline but still a negative one. It is not enough. Beyond it lies the ultimate path, which leads the person back into the world again but allows him or her to keep a secret interior detachment. The aura of intense mental peace that is felt in the presence of perfect mystics is not necessarily a sign of perfection, as the ignorant think, but a sign of successful inward-turned concentration. They consciously exert a mesmeric force on the disciples who sit passively around them. Sages, on the other hand, spend all this concentrative force in action intended to render real service to others while at the same time spontaneously and effortlessly also giving that which is given by the mystic to those who search.

The mental differences between them are too subtle and complex for the uninitiated multitude to grasp, but it is easy to understand the *practical* difference between them. A simple analogy will help us here. There are two kinds of electricity: static and dynamic. The first yields at best a single useless spark, whereas the second yields a flow of continuous useful power. The electric current that we tap for light, heat, and power belongs to the second category. Mystics, seeking to contract activities to a minimum, are like static electricity. Sages, seeking to render the utmost possible service during their lifetime, are like dynamic electricity.

Mystics, in their genuine need for solitude and silence, deliberately turn away from the world. Sages, in their compassionate consciousness of the darkness that overspreads it, deliberately turn toward the world. Psychologically, mystics are at the stage where they need to silence thinking and refrain from action in order to eliminate their disturbances, whereas sages have long passed that point and can afford to let both thinking and action have full free play without harm. Squatting mystics have to neglect the earth because they seek to soar in the heavenly sky; working sages have to stand upon the earth because they find it mirrors that sky! And whereas the first find God within and Satan outside in the world, the second find God everywhere. Mystics take pride in negligence of material affairs and in the half-heartedness with which they attend to material duties. Sages take pride in the efficiency and concentration with which they attend to material responsibilities. Mystics may self-righteously believe that paying proper attention to material life is the same as practicing materialism. Sages will sensibly believe that failing to do so is practicing foolishness. Thus the aim of philosophy is not, like that of mysticism, to turn us away from the world—quite the contrary. It wishes us to embrace life fully, but to do so with self-mastery, complete understanding, and disinterested helpfulness.

THE PHILOSOPHIC BALANCE

According to this teaching, it is the harmonious development and maintenance of a wise balance among three factors that, in their ultimate synthesis, yield realization of the philosophic ideal and thus make the sage. These are: mystical feeling, metaphysical thinking, and disinterested action. It is only in mediocre mentalities that these

tendencies disagree with each other. In superior souls they complement and help each other. Why is such stress laid on the last factor?
This is done not only because the integral—that is, physical, ethical,
and mental—welfare of humankind becomes inseparable from one's
own; not only because the waking state, that is, the world wherein
activity attains its climax, possesses a peculiar importance of its own,
but also because action is intimately connected with karma. Action
is the force that bestows the final propulsion to karma. We take the
last step to make or mar our ordinary life by our deeds, too. An old
Sanskrit text pithily explains the point thus: "According to his desire
is his habit of thinking, according to his habit of thinking he enacts
a deed, according to the deed enacted is his karmic lot in life."

Thought, however exalted, and feeling, however purified, are not
of themselves enough to perfect us in the realization of the Overself.
They are the seeds that must grow until they blossom into the flower
of disinterested action. Therefore, the philosophy of truth knows no
difference between theory and practice, for to it both are really one.
The student has every right to ask what practical purpose, what human
benefit, what tangible result is to be looked for from these studies. No
better test of a teaching can be devised than that simple one that Jesus
bade his hearers apply: "By their fruits shall ye know them." It is as
sound and effective today as it was in his own time.

These same points are thrown into high relief by the two world
wars and their aftermath. How can we remain indifferent or even
indolent, isolated in our own peace, in the face of a world suffering as
it never suffered before, if we really feel our mystical oneness with others? The answer, glibly given and gullibly accepted, is that the mystics
know best what they ought to do, that it suffices for them to work
on mysterious "spiritual" planes of being, and that it is sacrilege for
us to criticize them. But my answer is that the dreams become actual
when they leave the head and reach the hand and that in Buddha's

words: "A beautiful thought or word that is not followed by a corresponding action, is like a bright-hued flower that will bear no fruit." It is generally not within the average aspirant's competence to judge correctly who is or who is not a realized sage, but it is within his or her right to form a working and tentative judgment for the sake of personal and practical life. The mystical ascetic may stand indifferently aside, but the philosophic student cannot do so nor use the quest as an apology for inertia when faced with social responsibilities. The ascetic striving to detach from sense activity, the mystic seeking to turn his or her interests wholly inward, the atavist sheltering in an Indian ashram from the complex strain of Western life—all these are entitled by their standpoint, by their cloistral outlook that is so unsympathetic toward a practical and human teaching, to turn aside; but not those who would use their higher intelligence and master true philosophy. The value of such teaching proves itself best under the stern pressure of terrific events; it reveals its practical worth most when those who have mastered it have to withstand the impact of a war like the last one.

Philosophy cannot fulfill itself in the individual alone. It must work through society also. The interaction of both, in obedience to the higher laws of life, provides the field for its complete expression. This is a fundamental difference between the ancient and the modern teaching. The first usually separated the contemplative from the active life, whereas the second always unites them. The Christian, the Hindu, the Buddhist mystics usually had to withdraw from society's fold to pursue the inner life to its logical end, whereas philosophic mystics of today throw themselves ardently into the world arena to serve others. Everybody sees the historic struggle between the malefic and benefic forces in life, between what would arouse antipathy and stimulate selfishness among people and what would arouse sympathy and stimulate selflessness, but only the sage sees both this struggle and the concealed oneness beneath it. Whereas mystics, when they get a glimpse of this hidden unity of life, become emotionally mesmerized and physically immobilized by it and ascetically desert the fight in consequence, sages continue to take part and contribute help to the strengthening of the good forces. The disciples of philosophy should not hesitate to become a power in the world, utilizing that power not only for their personal benefit but equally and even more for humanity's benefit. Their social task is to adjust personal welfare to the common welfare and not to ignore either at the expense of the other. To do something worthwhile in life for themselves is the fruit of ambition, but to do something worthwhile for humanity also is the fruit of aspiration. It is the nature of manifestation to be ever-active; hence we cannot escape being involved in action of some kind. But what we can and should escape is being attached to our actions.

I am merely warning, as it were, less experienced people from the country, who are traveling for the first time to a metropolitan city, of the dangers that will confront them there and of the errors they are likely to make on the way. *I am not saying not to visit the metropolis!* Would-be mystics, therefore, ought not to become disheartened at the critical note that has deliberately been introduced into this essay as a protest against those monastically minded teachers who would arrogate the kingdom of heaven to chronic recluses like themselves and their followers, leaving us—the unfortunate captives of social circumstances and human duty—outside! Let them enter this path and pursue it assiduously, for it will well repay their effort; but let them take these criticisms as useful advice on what to avoid, ever remembering that mind is more than habiliment. If I have administered a shock to them, it is also true that those who faithfully endure must one day come to bless the hand that gave it. For they are being asked not to mistake a half-truth for a whole one. And I have sought to shame them into higher ideals of usefulness to suffering humanity.

THIRTEEN

What Can We Do for Philosophy?

WE ARE TOLD FROM time to time about people changing their religions or passing from one psychical outlook to another. We hear also of those who change a particular sectarian belief for a different one, or of those who go over from one religious fold to another. It is easy to understand that this is sure to happen in time, because most people and especially most women tend to be swept away by the popularity of an organization or institution, the glamor of a romantic personality, and the forcefulness of their own emotion. Hence they usually enter and stay within the religious or religio-mystical folds alone. Let us rejoice thereat, for this evidences that religion or mysticism is indeed amply nourishing them.

But life's upward movement does not and cannot stop there. One day it will also have to show some of the intellectual loftiness, the impersonal grandeur, and compassionate altruism of the philosophic goal. And although this higher path includes emotion, it does not depend solely on it. Emotion is fickle and naturally sways over to whatever happens to please it at a particular time. When the belief gradually shows up its deficiencies and the fold betrays its defects, the followers become ripe for change. But if they misplaced their faith once, they may misplace it twice, and even thrice. If they yesterday think something to be true that today they think to be false, where is the certitude that tomorrow they will not again reject this also and have a fresh idea of what is true? And if they can bring themselves to remember the strength with which they held those views that are now just as strongly rejected, how can they continue to trust their own judgment?

Time and experience may bring doubts and misgivings of this character to the mystically minded, but they can never bring them to the philosophically minded. For it is part of the duty of philosophic students to apply internal and external tests to our ideas. We must not only know that a thing is true but also know that the basis of our own knowledge is sound and irrefutable. Hence, the impression that philosophic truth makes on those who have comprehended it is so deep that it cannot be other than an enduring one, whereas the impression that any religious organization or mystical belief makes on the emotions of those who are attracted to it may fade and pass altogether when a different organization or another belief rises and supplants it.

Philosophy is not a different conception of life, facing and opposing other conceptions. It is too wide and too deep for that. None of the existing labels really suit it, none of the ready-made classifications really fit. The intellectuals or the mystics, the devotees or the doers who are exclusively absorbed in their own special path of life, permitting only those faculties that are engaged in it to function and repressing the others, are defective and inadequate as truth-seekers and consequently can obtain only defective and inadequate results. Philosophy alone avoids such one-sidedness and achieves the greatest and finest results. It cannot, by its very nature, reduce itself to party rivalry with any other teaching or worship. Its inmost heart is too loving, its practical attitude too generous, and its intellectual understanding too great for that to happen. Whereas each organization, group, or sect closes the door of heaven to every other one, philosophy leaves it open to all.

If we contrast the nature of true philosophy with the character of present-day humankind, we shall realize that the path of propagandizing is not the right one for us. We may drag the horse to the trough but we cannot make it drink what it regards as unpalatable. It is natural and inevitable that those who have an imperfect intelligence, impure intuition, faulty character, and selfish limitations should possess a worldview that is itself imperfect, faulty, and limited. Therefore the philosophic worldview, being the outcome of a deliberate discipline of thought, feeling, and action, refuses to oppose itself to any of the others—just as the philosopher refrains from interfering with the spiritual path of the unripe. The portal of religion is open to all irrespective of their qualifications, whereas the portal of philosophy is open only to those who possess a certain required degree of qualification. Anyone can become an accepted member of a religious body, whatever kind of character or intelligence, desires or aspirations one possesses; but there exists no philosophical body to admit one into its ranks. Anyone afflicted with the wildest hysteria, the most unbalanced neuroticism, can join a conventional church or even a mystical society; but such a person could not obtain acceptance by a philosophic teacher before he or she sufficiently restores balance. Before philosophy can serve us fruitfully, we must bring our whole psyche into a healthier balance or at least stop our emotions from running wild, our egotism from being dominant. We should not ask for spiritual illumination when our real need is for psychological treatment.

QUALIFICATIONS FOR PHILOSOPHY

Aspirants to philosophy first have to fit themselves with the needful qualifications. It is we who have to refine and elevate our characters, cultivate our intuitions, and conduct ourselves in a worthy manner. It is we who have to learn to study and think for ourselves. Thus, nobody is deliberately shut out from entry into philosophy. Let us gain the requisite qualifications and we will soon find ourselves inside; but because few are willing to pay this price, most people are to be found limited to the merely religious point of view and ignorant of the philosophical one. Hence nobody can convert anybody else to philosophy any more than one can convert a child into an adult overnight. All people must grow into it of their own accord, by the growth of their own character into readiness for it, by their own experience of life and practice of intuitive reflection.

Although so few are consciously seeking philosophic truth, the sages are not dissatisfied with the fact. They know it cannot be otherwise. They know that the uncomprehending dullness of the unevolved will give way only with the lapse of centuries, but it will surely give way to the unfoldment of the higher possibilities that even now lie latent in the multitude. Those who have had an opportunity to acquire the teachings of philosophy have had good fortune. But if they reject it because they are not ready, no blame can be attached to them.

It is a great fallacy, prevalent in religious and religio-mystical circles, to believe that people may change their characters overnight by some miracle-working spiritual means. What really happens in such cases is that a temporary vein of evil tendencies runs out and exhausts itself abruptly at the same time that a more durable vein of good ones shows itself. The belief that people can be changed overnight in moral character, motives, goals, and habits is naive. The fact is, they will embrace any -ism that appeals to their psychological make-up and temperament and their intellectual level, and that offers a medium for bringing about the change. But if they are not ready, then the so-called change will be on or near the surface, not really deep. It will be merely emotionalist and subject to a counter-change as soon as a new wave of opposing emotion sets in. The philosophic way also seeks to change people. But it sets up such an aim as an ultimate, not an immediate goal. For it guides itself by knowledge and wisdom; it walks by sight rather than by wishful thinking. Hence it is satisfied to do whatever it can to help people seek their higher selves, to gain a better understanding of the same and to aspire toward nobler characters than their present ones.

If all this is grasped, it will then be easy to grasp why ordinary religionists and mystical cultists eagerly set out to make converts whereas philosophy quietly sets out only to make its knowledge available to those who have become ripened to appreciate it— which are two entirely different activities. Philosophy recognizes the inexorable fact that people can be saved only individually, one by one. It has never expected many votaries. How could this be otherwise, when it expects so much of a person before it will accept him or her? For it expects humility, the consciousness of one's own ignorance; repentance, the consciousness of one's own sinfulness; deep aspiration, the consciousness of one's duty to attain the highest standards; hard intellectual work; constant meditation; and rigid moral conduct. Because philosophy offers what is more precious still, it demands a higher price from us. Even though World War II awakened many sleeping minds, it would still be foolish to expect a whirlwind growth of genuine interest in the quest of ultimate truth. A quantitative development is always possible, given some sensational and catchy turn of events; but as philosophic students we know that only a qualitative development is worthwhile, because it alone is deep enough to affect people's lives.

We must practice a wise reserve in such matters as the advocacy of truth, the conversion of foolish ignorant people into wise ones, and the spreading of these glorious truths in an inglorious world. We may be tempted, by the deplorable failure of religion in so many countries today to control the ethical conduct of humankind, to offer our philosophy as a universal panacea that will succeed in restoring everyone to ethical good health; we may like to play with utopian dreams of bringing heaven to earth overnight; we may even hope that the human race, more literate and better educated than ever before in its history, will rise eagerly to the offer of philosophy and accept it as the only faith fit for the twentieth century.

But to entertain such optimistic hopes is merely to deceive ourselves, and to act upon them is to invite failure. Philosophy demands keen, subtle intellectual acumen quite above the average even before its outlines can be understood, and humankind has an immense distance to travel before such full growth of intelligence is discernible. It requires a determined pursuit of truth for its own sake, which is little evidenced anywhere today. It makes no such blatant appeal as those religious and mystical systems that seek to bribe people with offers of emotional satisfaction for material gain. It is therefore and must remain a teaching for the few, not for the masses. Dreams of suddenly changing the social and economic structure of the world to a moral basis are faced with the unpalatable fact that human character cannot change en masse so suddenly and that until it is so changed all systems must inevitably be defective and unsatisfactory.

EDUCATING VS. PROSELYTIZING

It is the teaching of philosophy that humans are not to blame for rejecting it. A shallow mind, a weakened will, and a pampered body cannot let them do otherwise. Therefore, it desires to leave all people free to choose their own concepts of truth; to interfere with them by any attempt at proselytization would be to interfere with their real progress. If later through the test of riper experience they discover that their concept is unsuited or is a false one, the accompanying disappointment will enable them to finish with it once and for all and set them free to search elsewhere. Our duty is to make our knowledge available so that they need not grope or hunger one unnecessary day once the critical moment arrives when they are mature enough to perceive that here indeed is their bread of life.

These facts being comprehended, the futility of seeking a widespread reception of these ideas will also be comprehended. There is no need for dejection because we have perforce to walk alone or almost alone, however. Does this mean that we are to do nothing at all? No, it does not. We still have a duty. What is possible and practicable is gradual improvement. Competence must precede conversion and education must walk in front of propagation—in this field no other way is open. That is to say, we must train teachers in each of the populated continents of the world. We must use the printed word and make this knowledge available in the form of periodical publications that will gradually educate their readers. We must have a center of instruction by correspondence in each of these continents, too. We may even have to use the media for simple and elementary talks on our teaching—but here we shall have to be most careful to keep out the propagandist note and to retain the educative one.

The best way to preach your doctrines—meaning the most effective and lasting way—is first, to promote your own virtues, and second, to increase your own direct knowledge. Personal example and private teaching will be more effective in the end than aggressive public propaganda. People are still like sheep and walk obediently after the leader. It is our grand privilege as pioneers to hold

tomorrow's ideas today. These teachings have appeared in the world
in their present form and at the present time because they correspond
to the genuine need of a portion of humanity. They have appeared
because certain seekers of the West must now enter on a new phase
in their evolution. Philosophy's objective will be to give such guidance on vital subjects as can be obtained nowhere else. It is not that
the religious or mystical are asked to become philosophical, but that
the potentially or actually philosophical should not limit themselves
to religion or mysticism. Hence although philosophy is utterly uninterested in converting anybody, it is conscientiously interested in
stimulating those whose moral outlook, mystical intuition, and mental capacity could be widened without much difficulty. Only it does
so quietly and unobtrusively.

Both novice and sage may present the same truths with the intention of helping others. But whereas the first will be emotionally eager
to convert the other's mind to acceptance, the second will be calmly
indifferent to the result. And whereas novices will betray all their
eager missionary fervor, sages will not. They serve the gospel with
a manner that is so quiet and restrained, so hidden and subdued,
that only those who are ripe for its influence will be able to detect it.
Their efforts will be primarily to expound the truth rather than to
disseminate it. For their attitude is that of Confucius, who confessed:
"I do not expound my teaching to any who are not eager to learn it."
Propagation should be done with wisdom. For some it should not be
obvious, almost undetectable even; for others it may be very open and
frank. Sages consider well beforehand their own position and capacity, as well as those of the people they wish to influence, and then do
only what the circumstances call for and permit. Loud and ostenta-
tious propaganda is not for them. Silent and unobtrusive education
is. They follow the wisest course in spreading such abstruse ideas
and work intensively, not extensively, deeply among the few who

are loyally "truth's own" and not superficially among the many who are lukewarmly here today, gone tomorrow.

Their students live their own autonomous lives. They arise spontaneously, and come to them or their writings out of their own desperate need for inner guidance. Thus the sages' energies are channeled into purely spiritual lines instead of being wasted in merely physical ones. They will indirectly impart this knowledge through writings to some and directly coach others to carry on the work after they have gone. If they can create a loose, scattered, and unorganized group of individual students separated and spread out far and wide, in whom the finest ethical values, the loftiest intellectual standard, and the soundest mystical experiences will live on after they have vanished from the scene, even if each of its members strives and works in isolation, they will have done no less in the end for humanity than if they created a formal organization. And to the eyes of those who can look on life from the inside, they may have done more.

If it be true that the world cannot be converted to acceptance of such superior values, such lofty religious, mystical, and philosophic principles, and if it be likewise true that the world must be redeemed one day, what is to be the duty in the matter of those students who are the present-day bearers of these principles and values? Are they to stand helplessly by and let the impetus of evolution do everything? Or are they to propagate their ideas frantically and everywhere? The truth is that to indulge in over-pessimism is as fallacious as to indulge in over-optimism. They are to accept neither of these alternatives. They will rise to the level of their obligation by making a gesture toward their fellow humans that will not only combine what is best in both but also reject what is foolish in both. And this is to make available to humankind those ideas that have helped them, to let it be widely but quietly known that they do exist, to live faithfully up to them in actual practice so as to exemplify them as best they can, remembering that people will discover in their personal conduct the best account of their beliefs and the best echo of their knowledge.

This done, it should be left entirely to others whether or not they wish to accept. Students are not to waste their lives in forcing unpalatable food into the unwilling mouths of millions who are content merely to exist in mental apathy and emotional indifference, bereft of an inner life. Nevertheless, the opportunity to get this food must be presented, and in that our compassionate duty consists. It is true that truth needs no boosting. It can live on its own worth. Nevertheless, the fact of its existence needs to be made known. It needs its John-the-Baptists, for it sits remote and apart, silent and voiceless. It is not enough that the world sufferings have awakened the minds of many people and that the war, which has badly shaken people's feelings, has also quickly sharpened their wits. This awakening must also be directed into proper channels. Admittedly the higher teaching is, in its philosophic fullness, above the heads of the masses in their present state of evolution, although in the remote future it will certainly percolate through into their understanding. Most people are disinclined to struggle with doctrines that claim to give an insight into the mysteries of human, God, and Nature if these are too profound. But it is not above the heads of the intelligent or intuitive few among them, while its religious portion is well within the intellectual grasp of all and its mystical portion within the grasp of most.

A NEW HOPE

There is a new hope. In the past, philosophy could not directly reach the popular mind. Popular unpreparedness blocked the way. But today there has been such a development that some of it can directly filter down to the people. The unrelenting pressure of this crisis and the harrowing distress of war have abruptly aroused a number of people from their spiritual sleep. Mysticism, which they had—in common with most moderns—ignored as an empty abstraction, began to acquire vivid meaning and to assume personal reference. They started to take an interest in it, to seek information and to read books about it, to ask questions of or to discuss it with their friends. Mystical truths and practices have certainly carried some serenity to where it was most needed—to lands and homes that have endured the noise and tumult, the horrors and fears of scientifically waged war. There is now something that did not exist in pre-war days, an entirely new public for these teachings drawn from classes that have been brought by wartime experience into the ranks of seekers.

Under normal conditions, philosophic truth should be administered to a sick world in small doses, if on the one hand the patient is to be persuaded to swallow it and if on the other it is to be administered successfully at all. But today we are living under very abnormal conditions. If it was sinful to disclose the philosophic teaching in former times to the simple, illiterate masses and thus break their faith in the only spiritual standby they could comprehend, it is equally sinful not to disclose it today, when inherent sufferings and democratic educational developments have rendered them ripe for its consolation and instruction. Consequently the moment has come when it is the sacred duty of progressed students to disclose cautiously what will help their fellows in the present crisis and to quietly, unostentatiously, make these teachings available to all seekers; for the past eras of secrecy have served their purpose and come to an end. They need not expect to enlighten all humankind and would be mad to do so. But they may reasonably expect to enlighten a small nucleus around which the future will form steadily expanding accumulations under evolutionary pressure.

Those students who are alive in these dramatic epoch-making times should know better than to regard the fact as accidental.

Karma has put them on this planet, which means that the superior wisdom of their own Overself has put them here precisely at the present moment because it is charged with tremendous significance. That these nobler religious, mystical, and philosophic ideas will inevitably and eventually assert themselves sufficiently to influence the further course of humankind's mental history, is certain. Anything they can do within their different capacities and varying opportunities to accelerate such a process, it is their sacred duty to do.

Peace to all who read these lines!

My Initiations into the Overself

AFTER YEARS OF HESITATION and reluctance, I decided to chronicle my personal mystical experience. My first intention had been to write it in old age and to publish it anonymously or perhaps posthumously.* But I find that old age keeps on being before me, that instead of being more than half a century old I have simply lived for more than half a century, and that this task might as well be done now as later. There are still other chapters of this kind that will have to be written one day, but their concern is chiefly with cosmic mysteries rather than with personal experience, although the unveiling of those mysteries could not have happened except as a direct result of such experience. But since those subjects do not pertain to the present exposition, for they are on a plane that is more ethereal and less material, I have omitted them.

---

*Editor's note: This account was written when Paul Brunton was in his mid-fifties, but it was only published posthumously. More autobiographical material that includes his final twenty-five years is contained in *The Notebooks of Paul Brunton: Reflections on My Life and Writings*.

The reluctance to write about this subject arises partly because it touches private, intimate, and sacred moments, and partly because it will necessarily be so prolific in first-person pronouns that it will sound far too egotistic. Its very virtue may appear as its vanity. But I know from wide experience that such a narration will help those who are already seeking the Overself to recognize certain important signs on their own way, to learn where the correct path should lead them, and, above all, to confirm them in the necessity of hope. I believe, too, that it may give those who are not questers but ordinary people more faith that God does exist and more trust in the ultimate beneficence of God's World Idea. If it serves also in such ways, it can only do a little good to write and release this record.

Although a writer never really knows how much good or how much harm his or her work does (for the reports of its results are few and far between), if the aim is to serve, one need not be concerned about those results. Writers would do their best and find peace in the thought that fate will take care of them. So I follow the practice and counsel of an old Greek monk, Callistus Telicudes, who wrote: "One ought not to keep what is learned by Meditation, but one should make notes of it and circulate the writings for the use of others." This is why I communicate these inner experiences to those who might be helped, to those who might receive more vision of and more belief in life itself.

Before I reached the threshold of manhood and after six months of unwavering daily practice of meditation and eighteen months of burning aspiration for the Spiritual Self, I underwent a series of mystical ecstasies. During them I attained a kind of elementary consciousness of it.

If anyone could imagine a consciousness that does not objectify anything but remains in its own native purity, a happiness beyond which it is impossible to go, and a self that is unvaryingly one and the same, he or she would have the correct idea of the Overself.

There are not a few persons who have known infrequent occasions when their ordinary mentality seems to lapse, when their feeling for beauty and goodness seems to expand enormously, and when their worldly cynicism falls away into abeyance for a short time. The place may seem perfect for this experience, but it may also seem quite the opposite—such as a noisy metropolitan street. There are many other persons who have known the beauty of a great musical symphony and felt its power to draw the emotions into a vortex of delight or grandeur. Such persons can more easily imagine what this rapturous emotional mystical experience is like. But they may not know that under the ordinary human consciousness there is a hidden region whence these aesthetic feelings are drawn.

It was certainly the most blissful time I had ever had until then. I saw how transient and how shallow was earthly pleasure by comparison with the real happiness to be found in this deeper Self. Before my illumination the solitary scenes of Nature's grandeur usually served as my greatest form of inspiration. I could become so absorbed in admiring such beauty that I would feel swallowed up in it for a period of time and fall into a tranquil state. After my illumination I no longer became totally absorbed in such scenes. They remained something separate from me: I was detached from them. The emotional exaltation they aroused was less or lower than the peace and joy I felt in the Overself. Yet this spatial detachment did not prevent me from enjoying nature, art, and music to an even greater and more satisfying extent than previously. The detachment gave me freedom, release from some personal limitations, and enabled me to feel and understand beauty in a larger and deeper way. I even became more attentive to detail.

The glamor and the freshness of those mystical ecstasies subsided within three or four weeks and vanished. But the awareness kindled by them remained for three years. I then met an advanced mystic—an expatriate American living in Europe—who told me that I was near the point where I could advance to the next and higher degree of illumination and that, at such a period, most aspirants undergo certain tests before they succeed in gaining the degree.

He was right. I underwent the tests very soon after and failed in them—failed so miserably that I fell headlong down and lost even the spiritual consciousness I had previously possessed. The period that followed was a terrible one, a veritable "dark night of the soul" through which I had to struggle slowly and painfully for another three years. During all that period there was neither time nor capacity to practice meditation, nor was I inclined to sustain aspiration.

It is at times necessary to give questers a shock to show them what they are really like. This is usually done by friends, sometimes by enemies, and occasionally by the Master. It is always done by life itself. The experience is painful, but, if its lessons are sufficiently taken to heart, the debt owed to it is a large one. It arouses us to do what will save us from avoidable sufferings in the future by stimulating us to remove their causes within ourselves. One day I was faced with an unexpected event that gave me a tremendous shock. The emergency called for all the wisdom and strength and determination I could muster in order to deal with it. I succeeded in doing so and was drastically aroused in the process. In this way I shook myself out of the spiritual depression and, in a somewhat desultory manner, took up again the practice of meditation as well as occasional attempts at self-improvement.

This transition period was succeeded by another when I acted more resolutely and worked more diligently. I laid down a program for regular daily meditation, practiced even more intensively, and tried harder to improve myself than I had done for years. There suddenly came a feeling of impending momentous discovery. Six weeks later, I found myself plunged for two hours one evening (which was twice as long as the period allotted each day to the practice) in the deepest mental withdrawnness for me at the time. I felt I had come home after an all-too-long and dishonorable absence like a prodigal son. During that memorable session, I recovered once more the degree of consciousness that I had enjoyed in the earlier period of my quest, although there was more knowledge and understanding this time. I could see more clearly that there was a definite preordained pattern in my life and in the lives of others: all the chief events had some kind of inner meaning in them; all could teach some lesson that if learned would lead to spiritual growth. To discern these lessons, we have to develop a more mature emotional attitude in our relations with others and also a stronger character. We have to get ourselves out of our selves and look at each situation, momentarily at least, the way the other person involved in it looks at it. Then we have to seek true justice for all and not be selfish.

In the course of that evening's inner work, I found that my thoughts were being definitely directed along a certain course by some impulsion that was not altogether my own. It led me to retrace briefly the past history of my spiritual career and, especially, to examine carefully the point where I missed my step and lost my path. I analyzed the reasons for this mishap until they were perfectly clear and taken deeply to heart. Then I was led to build up imaginatively a picture of what might have happened had I successfully passed the tests. I was also led to see that each man or woman who had been brought by life into short or long association with me had borne a silent message or embodied a hidden test, or else was someone to be helped or served in a way that would reveal itself in time. That presence that was and yet was not told me inwardly how, through all the frustration and confusion that had filled the second cycle of my spiritual career, it had never left me but had remained beside me waiting for the time when my own efforts to find my way back would unite with its magnetic drawing power to liberate me. I was told that there was in this a great lesson—the necessity of hope—which I ought to communicate to the aspirants I would meet later who were spending fruitless barren years of spiritual seeking, and who were becoming discouraged at the lack of results.

Inexperienced travelers on this path often find that their early enthusiasm wanes and then the journey becomes tedious. For working upon themselves, changing, improving, and developing the moral, mental, and emotional material they must use is so slow an affair, so poor in visible results, that it tends to stifle buoyancy and enfeeble determination. Perhaps there will also be periods of harsh testing when resentment, doubt, or rebellion against the quest will appear within themselves. So I had to instill the lesson of never abandoning the belief that the struggle was worthwhile, of always trusting in the eventuality of grace, and of living in the memory of their past uplifted moments. Those who are intimidated by the quest's difficulties ought to be stimulated by its rewards. They should take to heart the truth that no spiritual darkness is a permanent one, and that at no time are they really lost, deserted, or fallen creatures. If their will weakens or their light clouds, it is an inevitable part or result of their imperfect nature as well as of their unfinished development. But it is also a condition that must right itself with further experience, evolutionary pressure, or unexpected grace.

When my meditation seemed to have ended, a great store of strength poured into me. Indeed, it was so overwhelming as to appear irresistible. I felt that every obstacle could be overcome by its support and help, and that I merely had to stretch out my hand to gain victory. Suddenly I saw a vision in which a duplicate of myself was pushing a huge boulder away from the entrance to a cave. I knew instinctively that the boulder was a symbol for the lower self and that the cave was a symbol for the Higher Self. I could feel a change working rapidly in my character and personality, bringing me closer to the ideal that I held. I succeeded at last in rolling away the boulder and, with that, attained a certain degree of self-mastery, which from that moment onward remained with me. I felt that I could never again fall below that degree, that it was no more possible to do so than it was for the hatched chicken to return to the egg.

I stood at the entrance to the cave and looked inside. I found it to be full of light, dazzlingly brilliant by comparison with the murky gloom outside it. The power to enter the cave was not given to me, only to stand at the entrance and gaze inside. I understood that the inner work necessary to gain this power would constitute the next cycle of my labors.

The vision came to an end and with it I realized that we do not become truly humble until we have first seen ourselves as truly great. The glimpse of our Higher Self throws a powerful light by reaction upon our darker one. We discover how simple, how ignorant, how weak, and how arrogant we are and have been. If the discovery brings us to the ground, it also stimulates us to resolve to remake ourselves in the image of the ideal. With the shaming contrast between the animal and the angelic, as well as between the human and the Divine, we are penetrated through and through with the need of imposing the higher will forcefully upon the lower one.

The years that succeeded this vision were years of development and growth. One of the most interesting new phenomena of that period came about occasionally when I was entering into or emerging from the deeper states of meditation. Out of the silent recesses of my being there came forth utterance—yet no form was to be seen and no one was there, nor did any vision come with it! This was the mystery—that speech came into existence without a speaker. It was the activity of vocal intuition, a presence that spoke to the inner ear and not to the outer. It must not be confused with the hearing of audible voices such as mediums and psychics are supposed to hear. It was nothing of that kind. This was my own Spiritual Self speaking to my human self. I suppose it was what the German mystics of the sixteenth century called "The Interior Word" and what the medieval saints of the Catholic church meant when they claimed that God talked to them. It was definite, commanding, forceful, insistent, and authoritative. If it gave an order, it gave also the power needed to carry out the order.

Yet it was not the intuition associated with everyday existence as an occasional phenomenon, for that is usually a mental first impression or a silent feeling. That intuition may well be the faint beginnings of this voice, which I like to call the Voice of the Overself.

I felt that I could put the utmost confidence in its guidance wherever it led me, even if it led directly to loss of every material possession, to sacrifice of every human relationship, and to the renunciation of every professional ambition.

The place where I heard this voice became ever after a holy sanctuary, an oasis of peace, and a citadel of strength to which I could return or retreat whenever I was alone, or whenever a crisis of the outer world was impending. People think too often that they have to travel to distant places for wisdom or teaching. They fail to recognize that it is not only within themselves—this wisdom or this teaching—but that it will never be found anywhere else. The echo of some other person's wisdom will never take its place.

To find the holy presence by withdrawing from the world temporarily into meditation was much easier than to find it while busy in the world. That was a different task. To go on from there until it became a fixed phenomenon was still harder. It may help others to learn how I did this. I had entered into a session that combined prayer with meditation. Although I assumed the usual physical position and it was the customary hour for the evening practice of meditation, actually I gave myself up to my feelings and spoke silently from the heart in fervent prayer. I addressed my words to the Overself and related how I had come evening after evening to this inner tryst, and I emphasized that it was aspiration and the attraction of love that had drawn me away from every other activity to spend more than an hour in this one. I admitted that an uplifting spiritual experience had often been the result, but I complained that the end of each session was the end of the experience. The next day had to be spent in ordinary consciousness like the day of any other person uninterested in the quest. I had taken up the practice of exercises in constant recollection as well as exercises in declarative muttering, but to no result; they were not my path. I still got so immersed in work or talk or whatever I happened to be doing that I forgot the practice and failed to carry it off.

It became obvious that if I depended on myself, on my own poor and feeble power, the effort could not end in anything but failure. There was no hope for progress unless the Overself came to my rescue and, out of its grace, brought about the desired state. I asked ardently for its help; indeed, I begged for it and lamented that life was worthless unless it could be lived continuously in that state. I carried on this one-way conversation in a lovingly familiar yet humbly beseeching tone.

A response came at last. I felt myself being carried down deeper into my inner being until a level of rich consciousness was touched. It required great intensity of purpose, great resolution of will, and extreme power of concentration to remain on that level, so I summoned up these resources and succeeded in remaining. After a while I was instructed by the inner voice to form a mental picture of a duplicate of myself at work, in talk, or travel, or in any other activity likely to be entered during the following day. In this picture I was to keep hold of the awareness in which I was now held and not to let my attention wander from it for even a minute. I was particularly guided to include such occasions or contacts where I was likely to be provoked by annoyance, irritation, overconcentration on work, and excessive physical activity into forgetfulness.

Thus the first step was to make the desired state come true in imagination. This could not be done without the fullest trust that it would do so, and without the fullest consent of my logical mind that it could do so. The second step was to identify myself imaginatively with the ideal state during the day as often as I could remember to do it, and during formal meditation periods as intensely as I could force the mind into doing it. In the first step I had to project a picture of myself as active in the outer world, to put forth a thought-form that would incubate for a period of time like an egg. I had not merely to think about that desired state from present conditions but also— indeed, rather—to think from it. I had to determine my outlook by it as if it were already an actuality and to imitate all the characteristics and qualities it had. I was not to gaze up to the idea, but to gaze down from it.

In the second step the ideal had to be knitted into me as if by a magic spell. I had to play the wizard and enchant myself into first seeing and then being what I aspired to become.

At first it was not possible to retain that peaceful state continuously. It would fade away intermittently. Both to prevent that from happening and to make the needed conditions to sustain its presence, the practice of this exercise in creative imagination became necessary. I found the exercise a valuable one for use in meditation practices of later years and so pass it on for the benefit of others.

Even then I knew that the effort required was too great for me, that imaginative power alone was too insufficient for such a result to be achieved without grace. If I had to depend on myself, on my poor little human self, the end of it would be merely an illusion that would one day be harshly dispelled or a dream from which I would one day rudely awake. The imagination by itself was not capable of bringing such an exalted state into actual realization, but the imagination plus grace was capable.

When the ego works on its own self, its willingness is reluctant and its power is limited. When grace works inside the ego, its participation is joyous and its power is unpredictable. Does divine grace exist? Orthodox theology makes an arbitrary fact of it and does not correctly present it. Yet it is reasonable in theory and verified by experience that it comes down to meet and mingle with human aspiration. But it is also a fact that such a desirable consciousness is not likely to happen if the aspirant fails to fulfill the conditions controlling its appearance.

On the day when its long-awaited dawn reddened my sky I certainly had no doubts that it was at work because I could directly feel its inner movements as soon as I started to meditate. I was perfectly aware of a swift change from the ordinary to the deeper level and of the inward pull, which are signs of its action and which repeated themselves many times in other meditations.

In the result, the state of divided being—the state of disunion in the heart—which had been my general state and which is necessarily the general state of all seekers, began to vanish. Instead of two opposing forces—the actual and the ideal—being ever at war within myself, there began to appear only a single controlling force. This led in turn to a great happiness, which made unnecessary all the constant searching for happiness in outside things, circumstances, or persons—a searching that is one of the causes of this self-division. I felt that the desires and attachments I had cared about so greatly, anguished over and worried for, were not important at all in themselves but only in the spiritual lesson to which they led in the end.

All the little desires, all the personal yearnings, are really God-desire.

At first this truth is unconscious, but with the growth of understanding it becomes conscious. It is then that the will turns around to start on the quest, and the desiring heart that had been looking and hungering for things outside itself starts to look within itself. In this emptying of self of fears and desires, the anxiety about the results of their activity is also emptied. At the same time there is the certainty that they will be taken care of in the World Mind's providence.

By carrying out these exercises and then consciously forming the habit of carrying their results into everyday life and routine, I came in time to keep the peace all day long. This was certainly a great reward for all the years of toil and effort that preceded it. But it also brought certain responsibilities to myself and to others.

Once identified with the cause of the true Self, how could anyone ever betray it by expressing any of the uglier traits and baser qualities that belong to the lower self? Once it is discovered that all that is noblest in every human aspiration comes from this sacred Source, how could one go along with one's ignoble tendencies?

Negatively, one could not raise one's hand or open one's lips to injure a fellow being. One could not be antagonistic to another even in thought. Positively, one has to practice an active goodwill toward all living creatures. Because of the sweetness that pervaded my heart, the world looked different and it was not difficult to restrain those ignobler tendencies. I was perfectly conscious of the fact that I was Spirit and that my neighbor, however outwardly repulsive he or she might be, was Spirit too. When I looked at anyone I saw the outer person as a mere surface appearance. Within it, in the heart region, there was a calm center of divine peace. It remained unchanged no matter how educated the surface self was and untarnished no matter how evil that self acted.

I no longer looked either for the worst in others or for the good in others but accepted them just as they were for that was the way they were. Never again could I condemn others too harshly. Each person I met was indeed a part of my own consciousness. I automatically and sympathetically identified myself with each or with anyone from whom I received a letter. I entered metaphorically into the shoes and shared the outlook, hopes, understanding, and, even, limitations of each person. My enemy was explained too: how and why he or she could not help being so. In this immense sympathetic sweep, I even ventured to justify him or her against me.

The time came when this attitude developed to an extreme. I did not know how to stop losing myself in the process of absorbing other persons into my own entity, so that they became a part of it, too often an incongruous part. What they thought or felt was reflected in my own consciousness like an image in a mirror. So if they told me something that did not correspond to the thought in their mind I immediately became aware of the discrepancy. It was sympathy lifted to a degree that amounted to empathy.

This faculty brought many unpleasant registrations to my mind and began to make life intolerable. Not until sometime later, when I had had enough of it, was I told and taught by the Interior Word that the condition was only a preliminary one and now needed to be brought under strict control. I was warned that I did not need to effect harmony with others on the plane of their ego. Help was given me for the cure of this condition but I, on my part, had to make a positive exercise of the will for many months and a definite withdrawal of attention from others as well. Gradually these phenomena disappeared until I became quite free of them.

Although I did not get any cosmic revelation in those days, I did feel in a general way that behind the universe there was extreme beneficence, that whatever happened had its place in the Infinite Purpose. No event was merely a chance one. The Infinite Wisdom was behind all human life and fortune. I felt that this applied just as much to so-called evil events and calamitous happenings if only we could interpret them correctly. This strongly intuitive feeling made me happy and I wanted to share it with others and to get them to rise above their own experience into it.

But paradoxically I did not feel any necessity to talk to others, even to friends, about these new experiences unless they themselves were seeking the inner life. On the contrary, it seemed sacrilegious to divulge promiscuously what had happened to me. So I deliberately concealed the fact of having these experiences. This was because I soon found that to preach truth to the mass of people was of no use. They could not grasp it and it was better to be silent about it except to those few who were themselves on the verge of the quest. I was taught inwardly, and confirmed by disappointment, that people stand on different levels of moral character, intuitive comprehension, and purpose in life, and I was warned to cease to try to proselytize, and to let the unready go their way while I went mine.

The supreme lesson of all experience must first be learned by undergoing experience itself. There was no other way at that stage. What could I do for those who would not seek themselves, but only objects outside themselves? They sought to impose more and more fetters on their minds and hearts; I sought to point out the way that could lead to a free and fetterless existence. The two directions were directly opposite one another. My time could be more usefully occupied with those who, having experienced the results of travel in the one, and satiated or disenchanted with these results, were at last ready for travel in the other direction.

I prayed to become a clear channel for the unhindered flow of inspiration, goodness, and truth to such persons, to those who were seeking for these things. As regards the unreceptive majority, I found it was more practical just to let the feeling of beneficence reflect itself through me to them as sincere goodwill and outward kindness. In some way and at some future time, the Spirit from which these two emanated would touch their subconscious being and affect them, help them, or uplift them when eventually it succeeded in rising to the conscious mind. The result might be slight or great, but it was certain.

During the years that elapsed, nothing dislodged me from those attitudes. If I would no longer try to push the truth upon others, neither would I let them push me out of it; and if they tried to, I could only silently smile at their foolish arguments. Experience itself was better than their arguments. I preferred to believe in the awareness that always remained with me than in the merely theoretical reasons for its non-existence.

It ought now to be made clear that these two initiations were mystical ones and not philosophic. They enabled me to see the inner meaning of my own life, but not of all life. They concerned the "I" and gave knowledge of the true Self. They did not concern the universe and the human relation to it. Those subjects belonged to the field of a philosophic initiation that came much later and was my fourth in line. That was an event that interpreted all other events. While still including the mystical initiation, there was blended into it the fuller perception of a Cosmic Knowledge.

I discovered that there are progressive degrees of the mystical initiation leading to progressive degrees of the cosmic one in turn. I have no experience beyond the first of the cosmic degrees. Yet even that slight unveiling taught me that the immense mystery that surrounds us will ever remain a mystery. The human entity is not competent to cope with more than a very limited degree of knowledge and still remain human. There is an iron ring around what it can know, a ring that we cannot pass beyond.

What I went through in these initiations may fairly be described as finding the true Self—that impersonal part of us that is covered over and effectively hidden by the personal ego. But the second time I found it in a very different way from that of the first, when the discovery had been tremendously emotional, excitedly rapturous, and ebulliently joyous. The second discovery was quiet, strong, and poised. This does not mean that it did not bring an intense glowing satisfaction: but all feeling was perfectly controlled by the sense of dominant will, of the higher purpose fulfilling itself rigidly. Indeed, I learned later that one of the tests of the greater enlightenment is the extraordinary calm in which it happens—a calm like the one that follows the violent monsoon storm in the tropics. To write that this inner peace is perfect is no literary overstatement or emotional coloring, but an accurate factual description. "Come unto Me all ye that are weary and heavy laden and I will give you rest" is still as true today as when spoken by the Christ-consciousness through Jesus nearly two thousand years ago.

In the first initiation I had only a vague notion of what was happening to me. This was partly because of its unfamiliarity, partly because I had little knowledge of the subject at the time, and partly because I lacked intellectual development at that early age. In the second one there was not only more understanding of the experience but better adjustment to it. Again, after the earlier experience, I found myself reverting to a child's simplicity, trust, and openness. But after the latter one there was a desire to add whatever discrimination, wisdom, and practicality that my experience and study had since been able to garner. These two tendencies existed side by side and seemed to accommodate each other without difficulty. There was no conflict between reason and intuition or between reason and faith.

Nor was this the only result of a paradoxical nature: there was another. When I lived in the Himalayas I felt especially during full-moon periods like the solitary inhabitant of an unpeopled planet. It is not easy even today to forget those unbelievable mountains where silence is total and absolute, where nature seems to be meditating and humans seem to be intruding. When I shut my door on the bustling world and retire first within my room and then within myself, it is as if I again enter into that still Himalayan world. There is utter silence within me. If I engage in work at the desk or go out into the bustling streets and mingle with people, it is as though a current is flowing steadily and incessantly through my heart—the current of that same inner peaceful silence.

Now I come to a metaphysical result of the second initiation. In the earlier one, I seemed to expand the ego with love and delight. In the later one, I seemed to attenuate it with perception and revaluation. Just before it happened I felt that some drastic and highly important event was about to develop. When it did happen the feeling was soon explained. There was a sloughing off of the old self, which was followed by a sense of immense relief. It was as if a tremendously heavy and burdensome topcoat had been thrown off my shoulders. The sense of being liberated was immeasurable. The ego's dominance was gone. I could see now how it had confined my thinking and dimmed my outlook.

It was simultaneously a kind of death and also a kind of birth—or rebirth—for in that life, which was Essence, I felt that the wishes, desires, attachments, and ambitions of the unreal self were futile, unnecessary, and vain. The entire existence to which they belonged was a dreamlike show, a passing cinema film. Those persons who were satisfied with such an existence were satisfied with a mere shadow of a shadow. They did not even suspect what the substance that cast the shadow really was, nor where it was, nor how to find it. This substance was the Infinite Life and Infinite Consciousness. It alone was real and eternal. Everything else was only a shadow-shape that merely reflected it. When later in the Near East an old adept of the

Hebrew Mystic Kabbala told me that its major text teaches that the Real Person lives like a sun in Heaven while only the shadow-person lives on earth, I immediately caught his meaning.

All the people I had ever known in the past or in the present, all the events of forgotten years as well as well-remembered ones, temporarily became nothing more than dreamlike figures in the mind, envisioned happenings in the consciousness, during this second initiation. If one of my own thoughts could suddenly become me, the thinker, the transformation would be something like the one that happens when the ego becomes the Overself. For I myself am nothing other than a thought in the Overself-consciousness.

Yet that discovery delighted me. I did not seem to care. My surface individuality was going or perhaps was gone, but, somehow, something mysteriously remained that was anonymous, nameless, universal, and absolute. That was the immeasurably important Essence of me: not the other with the petty desires and little idiosyncrasies, which had wasted my time for years and distracted me from the true significance of my life. Here, in this impersonal Being, I really belonged, lived, and found happiness.

After this it was easy to see why people welcome the condition of deep dreamless sleep. This is not only for the obvious reason of physical and mental recuperation, but also because it frees them from personal being, offers them an escape from the world and its care. This same freedom entered into knowledge of the Overself, but with a difference that the same happiness that is derived from deep sleep is here consciously enjoyed. Such happiness is really inseparable from awareness of the Overself. The reward of giving up the ego-sense is the ability to live in the deepest part of one's deepest being—the Overself.

Thus it became clear from both these initiations that it was all-important to rid the mind of the ego, or rather, of its crushing tyranny. This could not be the result of a single and sudden act, nor of years of disciplinary toil, but of a combination of the one leading to the other, of the Long Path leading to what is called the Short Path.

Although it properly belongs to my experience of philosophic initiation, it is perhaps interesting to note at this point that in the deep meditations accompanying that initiation I went through a stage where the ego's consciousness was annihilated so utterly and where pure consciousness, not centered or divided in any way, was so overwhelming that God alone reigned as I AM. There was then no duality of person and Overself, no hint even of the cosmic mysteries involved in the vanished world's existence.

And that is really the Truth: there is no second entity or power. There is only God.

Other Works
by Paul Brunton and
Related Works

EARLY WORKS, 1934–1952

A Search in Secret India
The Secret Path
A Search in Secret Egypt
A Message from Arunachala
A Hermit in the Himalayas
The Quest of the Overself
The Inner Reality (Discover Yourself)
Indian Philosophy and Modern Culture
The Hidden Teaching Beyond Yoga
The Wisdom of the Overself
The Spiritual Crisis of Man

PUBLISHED POSTHUMOUSLY, 1984–PRESENT

Essays on the Quest
The Notebooks of Paul Brunton
    1: *Perspectives*
    2: *The Quest*
    3: *Practices for the Quest: Relax and Retreat*
    4: *Meditation: The Body*
    5: *Emotions and Ethics: The Intellect*
    6: *The Ego: From Birth to Rebirth*
    7: *Healing of the Self: The Negatives*
    8: *Reflections on My Life and Writings*
    9: *Human Experience: The Arts in Culture*
    10: *The Orient*
    11: *The Sensitives*
    12: *The Religious Urge: The Reverential Life*
    13: *Relativity, Philosophy, and Mind*
    14: *Inspiration and the Overself*
    15: *Advanced Contemplation: The Peace Within You*
    16: *Enlightened Mind, Divine Mind*

COMPILATIONS FROM THE NOTEBOOKS

Meditations for People in Charge
Meditations for People in Crisis
What Is Karma?
The Gift of Grace
The Short Path to Enlightenment
Realizing Soul
The Wisdom of Paul Brunton Day by Day

COMMENTARIES ON THE NOTEBOOKS,
BY ANTHONY DAMIANI

Looking into Mind
Standing in Your Own Way
Living Wisdom

For more information about Paul Brunton, his writings, and the latest publications based on his work, visit **www.paulbrunton.org**. For reviews, excerpts, and a complete table of contents of his posthumously published *Notebooks* series, visit **www.larsonpublications.com**.

Index

Absolute, the, 159, 169, 173–76, 180

altruistic service, 117, 132, 137, 146, 167–68, 181, 195–99

Aristotle, 143

asceticism
  explanation of, 183–85
  inner purpose of, 111–12
  modified version of, 100–101
  politics and, 186–90

ashrams, 190–94

Augustine, Saint, 35, 162

Awhadi, 44, 131

Bhagavad Gita, 99–100, 154, 182, 196

Boehme, Jacob, 150–51

Brunton, Paul
  initiations into the Overself, 215–33
  works by, 234–36

Buddha, 41, 53, 56, 66–67, 68, 70, 106, 110–11, 136, 165, 196, 200–201

Buddhism, 41, 70, 98, 106, 188, 193, 201

Buddhist Bible, A, 193

Bunyan, John, 150

Chisto Tao Lun, 75

Christ, 26

Christ Self, 62, 153

Coming Down the Wye, 9

concentration, x, 8
  challenges to, 16–21
  nature of, 11–16

Cosmic Knowledge, 229

Dalai Lama, 188

dark night of the soul, 141, 144, 146, 218

Divine Atom, 43

Divine Mind, 3

Divine Self, 3, 17, 21, 63, 85, 104,
109

Divine Soul, 37, 63, 105, 109,
176

Divine Word, 44–50

Ecclesiastes, Book of, 40

ego, 26–27, 34, 45–46, 97, 102,
103–4, 156, 232–33
grace and, 225
surrender of, 116–28

Emerson, Ralph Waldo, 10

emotions, 7, 90–91, 203–4
cleansing of, 95–105
life of serenity and wonder,
113–15
meaning of desirelessness,
105–13

evil forces, 138–39, 140, 144, 147,
195, 226–27

Forbidden Land, 188

fourfold path, 37, 151

Gaudapada, 35

Gibbings, Robert, 9

God, 32, 39–40, 46–47, 53–54,
67, 149, 150–51, 171, 199,
233

Goddard, Dwight, 193

Godhead, 85, 169, 173, 177

Gorakh Bodh, 49–50

Gorakhnath, 49–50

grace, 23–26, 31, 35, 104, 121, 142,
149–58, 225

gurus, 64, 73, 82, 169–70, 189

heart, 38–43, 225–26

Higher Self, 12, 18, 22, 27, 29,
31–32, 33, 46, 48, 62–63,
95–96, 103, 119–20, 122,
124, 132, 134–35, 141–42,
144–45, 149, 152,
221

Himalayas, 230–31

Holy Spirit, 44, 142

humility, 17–18, 26–27, 119–20,
122, 152, 207

"I," 116, 118, 122, 229

I AM, 233

Imitation of Christ, The, 47

independent path, 80–88

Infinite Consciousness, 231

Infinite Life, 231

Infinite Mind, 182

Infinite Purpose, 227

Infinite Wisdom, 227–28

Inner Light, 41, 45, 86

insight, xi, 159–71

Interior Word, 44–50, 87, 222,
227

Isha Upanishad, 111

Jesus, 44, 53, 54–55, 56, 62,
    81, 85, 106, 114, 147–48,
    151, 154, 196, 200,
    230

Kabbala, 232
karma, 116, 124, 135, 137,
    153, 184, 195, 200,
    214
Krishna, 196

Lao Tzu, 181–82
Light on the Path, 98
living word, 44–50
Long Path, 233

Manu, 107
Matsyendranath, 49–50
Matter, 12, 39, 165, 168, 174–76,
    179–80
maya, 114, 179
meditation, ix–x, 192
    challenges to, 16–21
    character and, 97–98
    foundations of practice, 4–11
    importance of, 3
    integral path and, 36–37
    nature of concentration,
        11–16
    three stages of, 21–36
mentalism, 13, 106, 165, 174, 177,
    179

Mind, 42, 159–60, 164–65,
    174–79, 181, 197
Muhammad, 48, 53
Mundaka Upanishad, 40
mystics and mysticism, 1–2, 3–4,
    12–13, 76, 99–100, 167,
    183–85
    politics and, 186–90
    retreat and, 190–94
    serving the good of all,
        194–99

Nature, 41, 109

Overself, xi, 93–94, 97, 99,
    102–9, 119–22, 149–59,
    161, 165, 167, 170, 175,
    187, 214. *See also*
        Brunton, Paul
    Interior Word and, 44–50
    location of, 38–43
    meditation and, 15, 25, 26–27,
        32–33, 36–37
    self-reliance and, 61, 64–65,
        67–68, 69, 70–71, 74, 80–88,
        135, 141

Paine, Thomas, 187
Pali, 41–42
Patanjali, 113–14
Paul, Saint, 53, 153
philosophical mystics, 36–37

philosophy, 54–55, 57–60, 67–68,
90, 97, 116, 126–28, 167–68,
177–78, 192
balance of, 199–202
divergence from mysticism,
195–96
educating vs. proselytizing,
208–12
modern context for, 203–5
new hope of, 212–14
qualifications for, 206–8
society and, 201–2
Plato, 162
Psalms, Book of, 49

Quakers, 4

Ramakrishna, Sri, 64, 87–88, 114
Rip Van Winkle, 190

sages, 39, 52, 78, 79, 84, 87, 115,
170, 194, 196–99, 201–2,
210–11
Sahajananda, Swami, 109
Satan, 131, 182, 199
Shaikh Sharfuddin, 77
Shangri-la, 187, 188–89
Shankara, 10, 41–42
shekinah, 142
Short Path, 233
Silanka, 38
Singh (doctor), 49–50

Socrates, 65–66
Soul, 13, 23, 32–35, 46, 98, 101,
107–9, 132, 149
heart and, 38–43
recognition of, 2–3, 128
teachers and, 62–63, 80, 127
Spirit, 72, 107, 142, 147, 165,
173–75, 179–80, 226
Spiritual Self, 22, 41, 126–28, 216,
222
Sri Ramakrishna. See Ramakrishna,
Sri
Sufi, 10, 77
Supreme Reality, 159, 181
Sutra Kritanga Tika, 38
Svetasvatara Upanishad, 40

Tao Te Ching, 181–82
Theosophy, 60
Tibet, 11, 187–88
Tirumoolar, 41

Ultimate Reality, 174, 176–79
Universal Mind, 178–79
Ultimate Mind, 81
Universal Soul, 174
Upanishads, 40, 41, 49, 111, 156, 179

Vasishta, 195
Vivekananda, Swami, 114–15
Voice of the Overself, 222
Voice of the Silence, 49

Void, the, 81, 114, 165–66, 175,
    181–82

World Mind, 82, 165, 226
World War II, 190, 195, 200,
    207

Wu Wei, 181–82

yoga, 4, 13, 29, 39–41, 165, 190,
    197–98
Yoga Aphorisms, 113–14
Yoga Vasishta, 67

BOOKS OF RELATED INTEREST

The Heart of Yoga
Developing a Personal Practice
by T. K. V. Desikachar

Yoga Spandakarika
The Sacred Texts at the Origins of Tantra
by Daniel Odier

In the Company of Sages
The Journey of the Spiritual Seeker
by Greg Bogart

Tibetan Yoga
Principles and Practices
by Ian A. Baker
Foreword by Bhakha Tulku Rinpoche

The Path to the Guru
The Science of Self-Realization according to the Bhagavad Gita
by Scott Teitsworth

The Science of the Rishis
The Spiritual and Material Discoveries of the Ancient Sages of India
by Vanamali

Breathing through the Whole Body
The Buddha's Instructions on Integrating Mind, Body, and Breath
by Will Johnson

Hara
The Vital Center of Man
by Karlfried Graf Dürckheim

INNER TRADITIONS • BEAR & COMPANY
P.O. Box 388 • Rochester, VT 05767
1-800-246-8648 • www.InnerTraditions.com

Or contact your local bookseller